Houghton Mifflin · Reading

Horizons

Senior Authors
J. David Cooper
John J. Pikulski

Authors
Kathryn Au
David J. Chard
Gilbert Garcia
Claude Goldenberg
Phyllis Hunter
Marjorie Y. Lipson
Shane Templeton
Sheila Valencia
MaryEllen Vogt

Consultants
Linda H. Butler
Linnea C. Ehri
Carla Ford

HOUGHTON MIFFLIN

BOSTON

Acknowledgments begin on page 421.

Printed in the U.S.A.

ISBN: 0-618-24148-5

1 2 3 4 5 6 7 8 9 VH 09 08 07 06 05 04 03

Horizons

Theme 4

Animal Habitats

Theme Wrap-Up
Check Your Progress

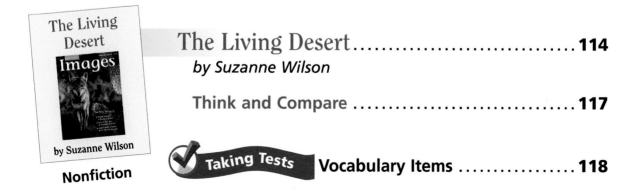

BIOGRAPHY

Voyagers

Voyagers

Theme Wrap-Up
Check Your Progress

FAIRY TALES

Smart Solutions

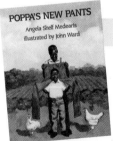

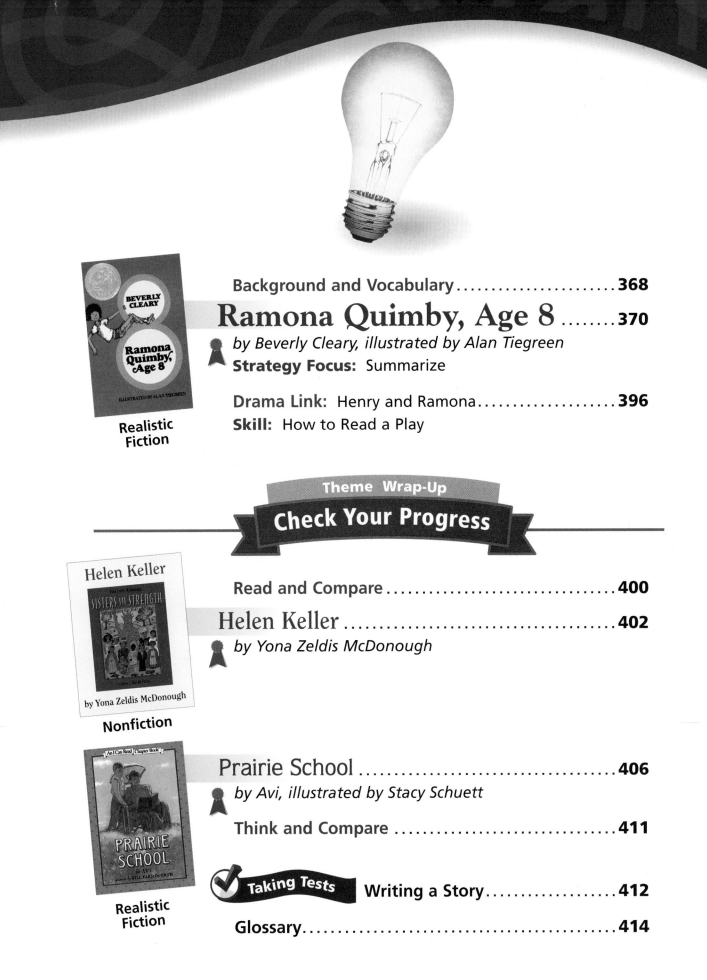

Animal Habitats

The Ways of Living Things

There is wonder past all wonder
in the ways of living things,
in a worm's intrepid wriggling,
in the song a blackbird sings, . . .

In a fish's joyful splashing,
in a snake that makes no sound,
in the smallest salamander
there is wonder to be found.

from the poem by Jack Prelutsky

Animal Habitats

with Bruce McMillan

All animal habitats are wonderfully complex, as are the animals that live there.

Our oceans are the largest animal habitat in the world. Oceans provide food for many animals. In the photo below, a humpback whale dives for fish off the coast of Maine.

The Guillemot (left) and the Razorbill (right) are sea birds. Like the humpback whale, their food source is fish in the ocean. During the summer, this Guillemot and Razorbill live in Iceland on steep rock cliffs. There are millions of these sea birds here. They all feed their chicks fresh fish up to ten times a day. That's a lot of fish. During the winter, these sea birds live on the sea, bobbing up and down on the ocean.

Chinstrap Penguins live in Antarctica. During the winter, they live on floating chunks of ice called ice floes. During the summer, they make pebble nests on land to raise their chicks. The penguins always live close to krill, the food they eat. Krill are tiny animals that look like shrimp. All year long the penguins swim and dive for krill.

Though our oceans are the largest animal habitat, our rain forests are home to the greatest number of animals. Of all the animals that live here, most of them are insects. This walking stick in a Caribbean island's rain forest is just one of the many kinds of insects that live in a rain forest. Rain forests are filled with plant life, food for the vast number of insects.

Deserts are another kind of animal habitat. This bird, a Greater Flamingo, makes its home on a Caribbean desert island. It feeds on orange-pink shrimp in a lake saltier than the ocean. The shrimp give the flamingo its bright color.

All of these animal habitats are amazingly unique places. In this theme, you will discover habitats that people and animals can share together.

Discovering Habitats

Bruce McMillan described some habitats where few people live. Are there habitats near your home? What are the habitats like? How do people and the animals in these habitats get along?

In this theme, you'll learn how people and animals can share the same space. It's time to travel around the world and discover how animals live. Enjoy the trip!

Internet

To learn about the authors in this theme, visit Education Place. **www.eduplace.com/kids**

Background and Vocabulary

Nights of the Pufflings

Bruce McMillan

Nights of the Pufflings

Read to find the meanings of these words.

e   Glossary

ashore

burrows

instinctively

launching

uninhabited

venture

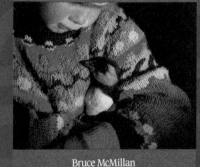

Iceland

Explore Iceland

Iceland is an island country in the North Atlantic Ocean. Only a small part of the island is covered with ice, though. In fact, the people and animals of Iceland enjoy all four seasons. And in June, the summer sun shines almost twenty-four hours a day.

Most Icelanders live in towns along the coast, so they know the ocean well.

In Iceland and on tiny, **uninhabited** islands close by, many ocean birds come **ashore** to nest in coastal **burrows**.

The birds know **instinctively** that the coastline is great for **launching** themselves out over the sea in search of fish. Many Icelanders enjoy watching these birds as they **venture** out from their nests. Find out more as you read the next selection.

Meet the Author and Photo-Illustrator

Bruce McMillan

When Bruce McMillan wants to see birds, he takes a trip around the world. He's photographed puffins in Iceland, penguins in Antarctica, and flamingos on a Caribbean island. You might not find such interesting birds in your own backyard. But now, thanks to McMillan, you might find them in your library.

McMillan received his first camera when he was only five years old. Working on books makes him "feel happy." That seems like a great reason to keep writing them!

Other books: *Penguins at Home*   *Wild Flamingos*
                  Summer Ice   *My Horse of the North*

Internet

Look for more information about Bruce McMillan at Education Place. **www.eduplace.com/kids**

Nights of the Pufflings

Bruce McMillan

Strategy Focus

What are the nights of the pufflings and why are they important? As you read, **evaluate** how well the author describes this exciting event.

Heimaey Island [HAY-mah-ay], Iceland
April

Halla [HATT-lah] searches the sky every day. As she watches from high on a cliff overlooking the sea, she spots her first puffin of the season. She whispers to herself, "Lundi" [LOON-dih], which means "puffin" in Icelandic.

Soon the sky is speckled with them — puffins, puffins everywhere. Millions of these birds are returning from their winter at sea. They are coming back to Halla's island and the nearby uninhabited islands to lay eggs and raise puffin chicks. It's the only time they come ashore.

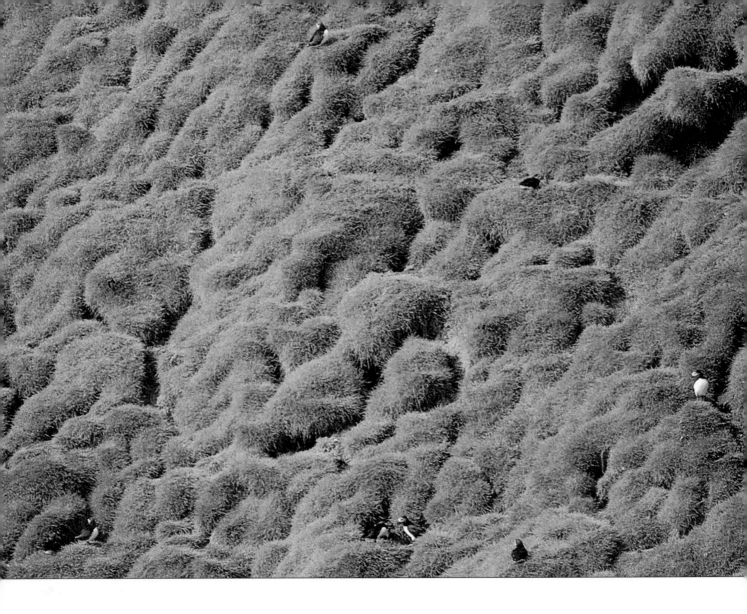

While Halla and her friends are at school in the village beneath the cliffs, the puffins continue to land. These "clowns of the sea" return to the same burrows year after year. Once back, they busy themselves getting their underground nests ready. Halla and all the children of Heimaey [HAY-mah-ay] can only wait and dream of the nights of the pufflings yet to come.

On the weekends, Halla and her friends climb over the cliffs to watch the birds. They see puffin pairs *tap-tap-tap* their beaks together. Each pair they see will soon tend an egg. Deep inside the cliffs that egg will hatch a chick. That chick will grow into a young puffling. That puffling will take its first flight. The nights of the pufflings will come.

In the summer, while Halla splashes in the cold ocean water, the puffins also splash. The sea below the cliffs is dotted with puffins bobbing on the waves. Like Halla, many puffins that ride the waves close to shore are young. The older birds usually fly farther out to sea where the fishing is better. The grown-up puffins have to catch lots of fish, because now that it's summer they are feeding more than just themselves.

Halla's friend, Arnar Ingi [ATT-nar ING-ee], spies a puffin overhead. "Fisk" [FIHSK], he whispers as he gazes at the returning puffin's bill full of fish. The puffin eggs have hatched, and the parents are bringing home fish to feed their chicks. The nights of the pufflings are still long weeks away, but Arnar Ingi thinks about getting some cardboard boxes ready.

Halla and her friends never see the chicks — only the chicks' parents see them. The baby puffins never come out. They stay safely hidden in the long dark tunnels of their burrows. But Halla and her friends hear them calling out for food. *"Peep-peep-peep."* The growing chicks are hungry. Their parents have to feed them — sometimes ten times a day — and carry many fish in their bills.

All summer long the adult puffins fish and tend to their feathers. By August, flowering baldusbrá [BAL-durs-brow] blanket the burrows. With the baldusbrá in full bloom, Halla knows that the wait is over. The hidden chicks have grown into young pufflings. The pufflings are ready to fly and will at last venture out into the night. Now it's time.

It's time for Halla and her friends to get out their boxes and flashlights for the nights of the pufflings. Starting tonight, and for the next two weeks, the pufflings will be leaving for their winter at sea. Halla and her friends will spend each night searching for stranded pufflings that don't make it to the water. But the village cats and dogs will be searching, too. It will be a race to see who finds the stray pufflings first. By ten o'clock the streets of Heimaey are alive with roaming children.

In the darkness of night, the pufflings leave their burrows for their first flight. It's a short, wing-flapping trip from the high cliffs. Most of the birds splash-land safely in the sea below. But some get confused by the village lights — perhaps they think the lights are moonbeams reflecting on the water. Hundreds of the pufflings crash-land in the village every night. Unable to take off from flat ground, they run around and try to hide. Dangers await. Even if the cats and dogs don't get them, the pufflings might get run over by cars or trucks.

Halla and her friends race to the rescue. Armed with their flashlights, they wander through the village. They search dark places. Halla yells out "puffling" in Icelandic. "Lundi pysja!" [LOON-dih PIHS-yah]. She has spotted one. When the puffling runs down the street, she races after it, grabs it, and nestles it in her arms. Arnar Ingi catches one, too. No sooner are the pufflings safe in the cardboard boxes than more of them land nearby. "Lundi pysja! Lundi pysja!"

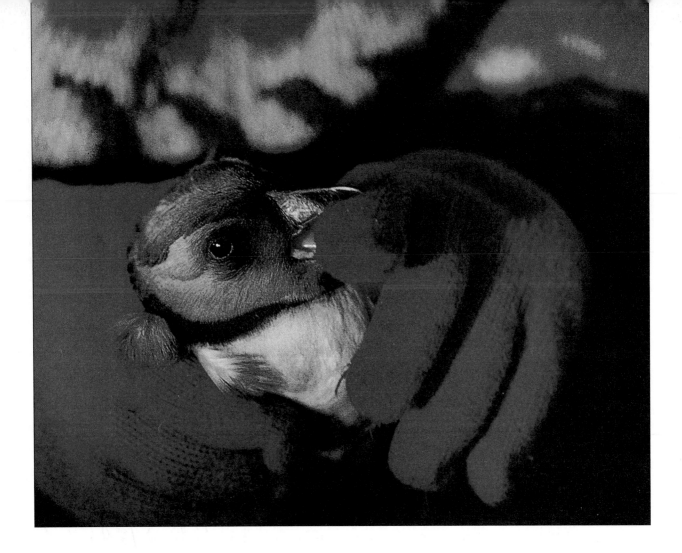

For two weeks all the children of Heimaey sleep late in the day so they can stay out at night. They rescue thousands of pufflings. There are pufflings, pufflings everywhere, and helping hands too — even though the pufflings instinctively nip at helping fingers. Every night Halla and her friends take the rescued pufflings home. The next day they send their guests on their way. Halla meets her friends and, with the boxes full of pufflings, they hike down to the beach.

It's time to set the pufflings free. Halla releases one first. She holds it up so that it will get used to flapping its wings. Then, with the puffling held snugly in her hands, she counts "Einn–tveir–ÞRÍR!" [AYT–TVAYRR–THRREER] as she swings the puffling three times between her legs. The last swing is the highest, launching the bird up in the air and out over the water beyond the surf. It's only the second time this puffling has flown, so it flutters just a short distance before safely splash-landing.

Day after day Halla's pufflings paddle away, until the nights of the pufflings are over for the year. As she watches the last of the pufflings and adult puffins leave for their winter at sea, Halla bids them farewell until next spring. She wishes them a safe journey as she calls out "goodbye, goodbye" in Icelandic. "Bless, bless!"

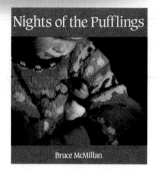

Nights of the Pufflings

Bruce McMillan

Think About the Selection

1. Why do you think puffins are called "clowns of the sea"?

2. Why do you think the children return the pufflings to the sea instead of keeping them as pets?

3. What would you like best about visiting Heimaey Island during the nights of the pufflings? Why?

4. What makes the nights of the pufflings exciting? Describe an exciting event that you wait for every year.

5. Give some reasons why Bruce McMillan might have wanted to write a book about the pufflings.

6. **Connecting/Comparing** How did humans cause the pufflings' habitat to change? Describe other ways people could have solved the pufflings' problem.

Persuading

Write a Travel Brochure

Welcome to Heimaey Island

Create a brochure for travelers who might want to visit Heimaey Island. Describe the scenery and animals of the island. Then write about the activities visitors might enjoy there. Draw pictures to illustrate your brochure.

Tips

- To get started, list everything you want your brochure to describe.
- Look at real travel brochures for ideas.

Draw a Habitat Diagram

Make a diagram of Heimaey Island. Label the cliffs, sea, and village. Then draw arrows to show where a puffin travels as it grows from a baby bird to a flying adult. Number the steps of the puffin's journey. Write a short description of each step.

Study a Photograph

Look closely at the photos of puffins on pages 25 and 26. Then use the photos to write a description of a puffin. Describe how the puffin looks from top to bottom. Give lots of details about the puffin's head, beak, body, and feet.

Bonus To test how good your description is, give it to someone who has never seen a puffin. Ask that person to draw a puffin based on your description.

Internet

Post a Review

How well do you think the author told this story? Do you like his photographs? Share your opinions by writing a review for Education Place. **www.eduplace.com/kids**

Skill: How to Use the SQRR Plan

❶ Look at, or **survey**, the title, headings, captions, and pictures.

❷ Ask yourself **questions** about what you surveyed.

❸ Look for answers to your questions as you **read**.

❹ After reading, **review** your questions to see if you can answer them.

BIG-APPLE BIRDING

Hundreds of different kinds of wild birds in New York City? We thought our teacher was bonkers!

by Radha Permaul, with Arthur Morris
photos by Arthur Morris

36

"No way!" I said to my teacher, Mr. Morris. He had just told us that there are hundreds of different kinds of birds in the Big Apple. (That is what people sometimes call New York City.) Sure, I'd seen a few kinds in my neighborhood. But *hundreds* of kinds? Nah.

Then Mr. Morris surprised us. He asked, "How would you kids like to go birding with me sometime — you know, watch birds with binoculars?" I was really excited, because I like to go on trips with my friends.

Central Park Hike

Early on a bright spring day, the five of us took the subway to New York's Central Park. The first thing we noticed were robins tugging worms from the damp soil. Then we started to see lots of beautiful warblers (tiny, colorful birds).

Mr. Morris said that some of the birds we saw don't stay in Central Park. "Many of them are just stopping here to feed and rest," Mr. Morris explained. "Then they'll keep flying north. Some will go another thousand miles into Canada."

Now *that* was totally amazing!

That's me (Radha) with Nelson and Tanya behind me. We were amazed to see a really cool *hooded warbler* and a *white-throated sparrow* (next page) right in New York City!

hooded warbler

white-throated sparrow

scarlet tanager

glossy ibis

Where's That Bird?

"Listen up, kids," Mr. Morris said in a serious voice. "Help me look for something really special."

He was pointing in a book to a red and black bird called a scarlet tanager. "This guy flies all the way from South America and sometimes stops to rest in the park."

We saw lots of cool birds, but no scarlet tanagers. Then, as we crossed a little brook, Jamie whispered, "I just saw something red in that tree.... There it is on that branch in the sun. See?"

I raised my binoculars and knew it had to be a scarlet tanager. Its red feathers were brighter in real life than they were in the picture! "Wow, good going, Jamie," Mr. Morris said with a grin.

Jay Bay . . . Hooray

A couple of weeks later we went to Jay Bay. That's what Mr. Morris calls the Jamaica Bay Wildlife Refuge. We followed a trail to the West Pond.

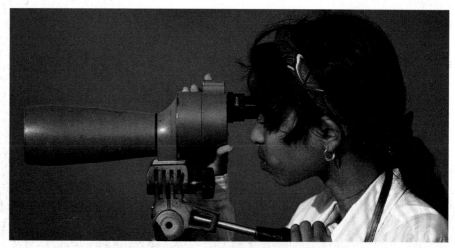
I watched a *glossy ibis* through a spotting scope.

I kept hearing a strange-sounding bird call: "Kong-ka-*ree*, kong-ka-*ree*!" I really wanted to know what was making the sound. Finally, I saw a black bird with red on its wings — and it was singing that strange song.

Mr. Morris handed me his detective book — a bird book called a field guide. It was my job to track down the bird's name. I found a page full of dark birds, and there it was. "Got it," I said. "It's a red-winged blackbird."

Everything was so pretty that my neighborhood seemed a thousand miles away. And I was beginning to think that there really could be hundreds of different kinds of birds in the Big Apple.

City Birding

If you live in a big city and want to watch birds, here's what you can do: Ask at a nature center or science museum where the best birding places are. Next, go to a library to get a field guide. Study it. Borrow some binoculars. Then visit the hot birding spots with your parents or friends.

A Research Report

A research report presents facts about a topic and uses details to support the facts. Use this student's writing as a model when you write a research report of your own.

Glue

Loggerhead Turtles

Topic sentences introduce the report.

The loggerhead turtle is a reptile. It has a thick, straight neck, wrinkled skin, and a hard shell. The head is wide, and has a beak formed by two hooked jaws. Even though the loggerhead turtle has a shell for protection, it is still an endangered animal.

A loggerhead turtle is a large sea turtle, and it has flippers to swim and to get around. Its skin is light green to dark green, and its shell is a reddish brown. An adult loggerhead turtle can weigh up to 880 pounds and is about three and one-half feet long. It has very strong jaws, which it uses to crack the hard bodies of the clams, conches, and crustaceans that it eats.

The loggerhead turtle lives in the subtropical zones of the Atlantic Ocean, the Mediterranean Sea, the Black Sea, and the Pacific and Indian Oceans. In the United States, it usually visits the coasts of Florida and South Carolina.

When the female reaches the coast, she comes onto the shore to lay eggs. She digs a hole to store about 100 eggs. The female can lay between 64 and 200 eggs. The baby turtles that hatch from the eggs are about four and one-half inches long. When they are old enough, they come out of the sand and head for the ocean.

Here are some baby turtles heading for the ocean.

A good **conclusion** sums up the report.

Pollution, hunters, oil spills, and shrimp nets are some of the turtle's enemies. People can protect the turtles by being careful about throwing away plastic bags or soda-can holders. If these items are thrown away carelessly, they cause the turtles to choke. People can also help to save the baby loggerhead turtles by putting up fences to protect them when they are heading to the ocean.

Loggerhead turtles have been on Earth a long time. Protecting them can get them off the endangered list.

Here is someone helping to protect a turtle nest.

List of Sources

The Grolier Student Encyclopedia of Endangered Species. Vol IX. 1995.

Endangered Wildlife of the World. Vol 9. Marshall Cavendish Corp. 1993.

Gibbons, Gail. *Sea Turtles.* Holiday House, New York. 1995.

> The **List of Sources** tells where the facts came from.

Meet the Author

Mark F.

Grade: three
State: Massachusetts
Hobbies: soccer and football
What he'd like to be when he grows up: a football player or a dentist

Background and Vocabulary

SEAL SURFER
MICHAEL FOREMAN

Seal Surfer

Read to find the meanings of these words.

e · Glossary

basked

buffeted

horizon

quay

surf

swell

swooped

At the Seashore

The seashore is the place where the land meets the ocean. There are many ways to enjoy the seashore. After you have **basked** in the warm sun, you can **surf** the big waves or float on an ocean **swell**. On a brisk day, turn toward the sea and be **buffeted** by the rough winds.

Along some shores, like the one in the story *Seal Surfer*, you can enjoy more than the ocean. Look for sea birds that have **swooped** down to catch fish. Walk along the **quay**, where you can see ships docked in the harbor. At the end of the day, watch the sky fill with dazzling colors as the sun sets below the **horizon**. Whatever you do, you'll have a great day at the seashore.

Meet the Author and Illustrator

Michael Foreman

From his home in England, Michael Foreman has traveled to North America, Europe, Africa, Asia, and Australia — and crossed many oceans to do so. All these journeys have given him many ideas for his stories and pictures.

Foreman doesn't always travel so far for ideas, though. As he explains, "You don't need to cross the ocean to find ideas — just look across the kitchen table at your family, or in the attic and the memories of your childhood. . . . You don't need to travel here, there, and everywhere. But I'm awfully glad I did!"

OTHER BOOKS:

Jack's Fantastic Voyage
Peter's Place (by Sally Grindley)
The Tiger Who Lost His Stripes
   (by Anthony Paul)

Internet

Take a trip of your own and visit Education Place to learn more about Michael Foreman.
www.eduplace.com/kids

MICHAEL FOREMAN

SEAL SURFER

This is the story of an unusual friendship between a boy and a seal. As you read, pause every few pages to **summarize** the events in the story.

SPRING

One day in early spring an old man and his grandson, Ben, carefully climbed down to a rocky beach. They were looking for mussels.

As Ben searched he noticed a slight movement among the rocks. Then he saw the seal. It was difficult to see her body against the rocks, except for a smudge of red on her belly.

"Look, Granddad!" Ben cried. "The seal is injured."

"Don't get too close," warned Granddad. They watched
the seal from a distance.

The seal looked quite calm, lying still in the morning
sun, and after a while Ben started hunting for mussels again.

When he next looked up at the seal, he saw a flash of
white. A newly born seal pup nuzzled her mother.

"Quick, Granddad," whispered Ben. "Let's get some fish
for the seals."

As the spring days lengthened, Ben and his granddad often watched the seal family from the cliff top. The pup's white coat molted and she became the color of the rocks. Sometimes she moved to the water's edge to watch her mother fish. As she basked in the warm sun, she kept an eye on Ben and his granddad.

SUMMER

In early summer Ben watched as the mother seal pushed her pup off the rocks and into the sea. The shock of the cold water made the young seal panic. The water closed over her head. She pushed upward with her tail and flippers until her head burst through the surface.

Her mother plunged into the water, and together they swam around and around — diving, twisting, corkscrewing into the depths. When the seal pup broke through the water's surface, she heard the boy cheer.

AUTUMN

The summer days faded. One evening Ben went down
to the harbor to meet his granddad, who was returning
from a day's fishing. Granddad's old pickup truck sat
with the door open and the radio on. The music of
Beethoven [BAY-toh-vuhn] filled the air.

Granddad stared into the water. A whiskery face stared
back at him like a reflection in the moonlit mirror of the harbor.
Granddad tossed the seal a fish — and then another.
Ben watched as the mirror dissolved, reformed, and then
dissolved again as they all shared the music of Beethoven.

WINTER

While the wet winter winds buffeted the boy on his way to school, the young seal learned the lessons of the sea.

The seal loved to swim far from home, exploring the coast. She learned to fish by swimming deep and looking up to see the fish outlined against the sky.

She slept at sea, floating upright like a bottle, with just her nose above the surface. Best of all she loved to haul herself up onto the rocks with other young seals to feel the sun and wind on her skin.

But one day the wind rose suddenly into a full-blown gale. Rain and mountainous waves wrenched great rocks from the cliffs. The young seals dived deep, trying to escape falling boulders. But even in the sea they were in danger. Some seals were dashed against the rocks by the waves.

SPRING

The warmth of spring brought wildflowers and Ben and his granddad to the cliffs once more. But there was no sign of the young seal.

"She must have died in the winter storms," said Ben.

But sometimes the mother seal still came to the harbor for an evening of fish and music.

SUMMER

As spring warmed into summer, Ben went every Saturday to Surf School. He was a strong swimmer, and after much practice he and the other new surfers were ready to catch some waves.

One sunny day Ben lay on his board as it rose and fell on the gently rocking swell. Suddenly he was aware of a quick movement in the water. A dark shape swooped under the board. The gleaming face of the young seal popped up beside his own. Ben was elated. "You're alive!" he called, grinning.

The sea gathered itself for some big waves. The dark green walls of water lined up along the horizon. The seal sensed the movement of the water. Ben and the seal let the first two waves pass, then together they rode the third huge, rolling wave toward the shore.

All afternoon Ben and the seal surfed together. Then just as quickly as she had appeared, the seal was gone. Ben waited awhile and then let the next good wave carry him to the sand.

The next day the tide was perfect and the young seal was back. Again Ben and the seal surfed side by side.

Ben could not take his eyes off the seal as she flashed through the water. As he concentrated on watching her, the wave he was riding suddenly broke and plunged him headfirst off his board. He somersaulted through the surf and struck a rock. The water, thick with sand, filled his nose and mouth. His body was pulled deeper and deeper. He was sinking into darkness.

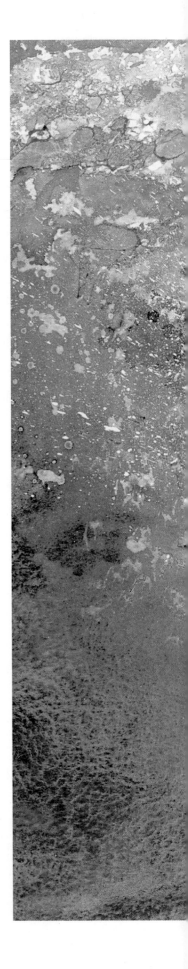

Then he felt a different sensation. His body was forced upward. Sunlight shone through the water onto Ben's face as the seal pushed his body up. With a final heave she flipped Ben onto his board. He held on, and the next wave carried him to the shore. His friends crowded around to make sure he was all right. Once he caught his breath, Ben felt fine.

The next afternoon, and for the rest of the long, hot summer, Ben surfed with the seal.

WINTER

The wonderful summer and gentle autumn were followed by the worst of winters. The storms smacked the rocks and churned up the sand and stones. The beach was deserted. No seals came there.

SPRING

When the next spring brought the wildflowers to the cliffs, it brought Ben but not his grandfather. The boy and his friends ventured far along the cliffs, but they could find no sign of the seals.

SUMMER

As the evenings grew lighter toward the start of summer, Ben began fishing from the quay, as his granddad had done before him. One evening as he watched the still water, two shiny heads broke through the surface. Ben cheered as he saw the once young seal — now as whiskery as Granddad — with her young pup.

Ben smiled. He knew, then, that he would ride the waves with the seals that summer and every summer.

And maybe one day he would lie on the cliff tops with his own grandchildren and together they would watch the seals.

SEAL SURFER

Think About the Selection

1. Compare how the characters and the seals change during the story.

2. Why do you think Ben enjoys watching the seals?

3. Is it believable that a seal could rescue a surfer from drowning? Why or why not?

4. What kinds of activities might Ben do someday with his own grandchildren?

5. Ben likes to visit the cliffs. Describe an outside place that you like and how it changes with the seasons.

6. **Connecting/Comparing** Compare the animal habitat in *Seal Surfer* with the one in *Nights of the Pufflings.*

Expressing

Write an Acrostic Poem

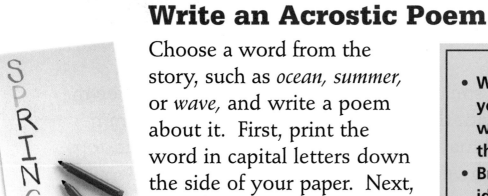

Choose a word from the story, such as *ocean, summer,* or *wave,* and write a poem about it. First, print the word in capital letters down the side of your paper. Next, beside each letter, write a sentence or phrase that begins with that letter.

> **Tips**
> • Write about what you feel or think when you hear the word.
> • Brainstorm several ideas for each line. Then choose the best one.

Math

Calculate Calendar Time

The story takes place over two-and-a-half years. How many months is that in all? Begin by finding out how many months are in one year. Then write a number sentence to help find the answer.

Bonus How many weeks is that in all? How many days?

Music

Listen to Beethoven

Ben's grandfather plays music written by Beethoven. The mother seal seems to like the music. Do you? Listen carefully to a recording of music by Beethoven. Draw a picture or write a paragraph to show how the music makes you feel.

Ludwig van Beethoven

Internet

Go on a Web Field Trip

Explore animal habitats around the world when you connect to Education Place. **www.eduplace.com/kids**

I Work in the Ocean

A Profile of an Underwater Photographer

by Kristin Ingram

Norbert Wu's coworkers are fish. Instead of putting on a business suit and driving to an office, this underwater photographer puts on scuba gear and dives into the ocean. Norbert travels around the world to photograph all kinds of strange, beautiful, and even dangerous creatures. He'll photograph just about anything that lives underwater, but he especially enjoys difficult projects.

A school of ▶ silverside minnows in the Red Sea

▲
Norbert Wu with his camera

▲ **Hundreds of hammerhead sharks near Isla del Coco, Costa Rica**

On a shoot near Isla del Coco, Costa Rica, he held his breath while kicking furiously to swim beneath a huge school of hammerhead sharks. He had to wait until after he took the photo to exhale, because the cloud of bubbles would have scared the sharks away.

In the Bahamas Norbert had to swim quickly to keep up with a group of wild dolphins. They zipped and dove while playing tag and passing seaweed back and forth.

▲ **A candy-cane starfish near Borneo**

67

Norbert doesn't always race around underwater. Sometimes he must keep as still as possible so he won't startle a shy animal. Once in the Caribbean Sea he found a blenny living in a hole in a coral reef. Whenever he tried to photograph it, the fish popped back into its hole. Finally it got used to him and let him get close enough to take the shot.

Norbert's work isn't always dangerous and exciting. He spends lots of time in his California office doing paperwork and fixing up equipment. The watertight cases, called housings, that protect his cameras must be free of leaks.

Underwater photos need strong lighting, so Norbert attaches strobe lights to bendable arms on the housings. When he tests his equipment in Monterey Bay, it looks as if he's carrying a miniature spaceship. Curious harbor seals and sea lions follow him around. Sometimes they even nuzzle Norbert's camera.

How did Norbert become an underwater photographer? As a boy his favorite summer activities were swimming and scuba diving. He continued these hobbies through college and added underwater photography to the list.

▼ **Norbert meets a curious seal.**

▲ **The blenny Norbert finally photographed**

▲ **A school of fairy basslets crowds around corals in the Red Sea.**

During his years at Scripps Institute of Oceanography in San Diego, Norbert discovered that he had a talent for taking good underwater photos. And he realized that with them he could help people see and understand the ocean the way he did.

Although Norbert has seen marvelous sights, he has also witnessed many sad things. Pollution has damaged fragile ecosystems such as coral reefs, and overfishing has reduced the populations of some oceans. By taking pictures that show how interesting and beautiful sea animals are, Norbert hopes he'll inspire people to help protect them.

Perhaps one day you, too, will dive into Norbert's underwater world and share his delight at its wonders. Even if you prefer to stay dry, you can always count on him to bring back incredible photographs.

HARRIET PECK TAYLOR

Two Days in May

PICTURES BY LEYLA TORRES

Two Days in May

Read to find the meanings of these words.

e Glossary

grazing

population

starve

surrounding

territory

wander

Deer

Like all animals, deer need food and shelter to live. They can find what they need in many different habitats around the world. Deer live on every continent except Antarctica.

Deer do not make homes in dens or nests. They **wander** through a large area or **territory**, searching for food and resting whenever they find a safe spot.

Sometimes there are too many deer in one place. If the deer **population** grows too large, some of them may wander into new areas. They may even find their way into towns and cities **surrounding** their usual territory. This is what happens in the story you are about to read.

Deer eat almost any kind of ▶ **plant. They enjoy grazing on flowers, grass, buds, leaves, and twigs.**

As long as they can find a wooded or grassy area, deer will never starve.

Selection 3

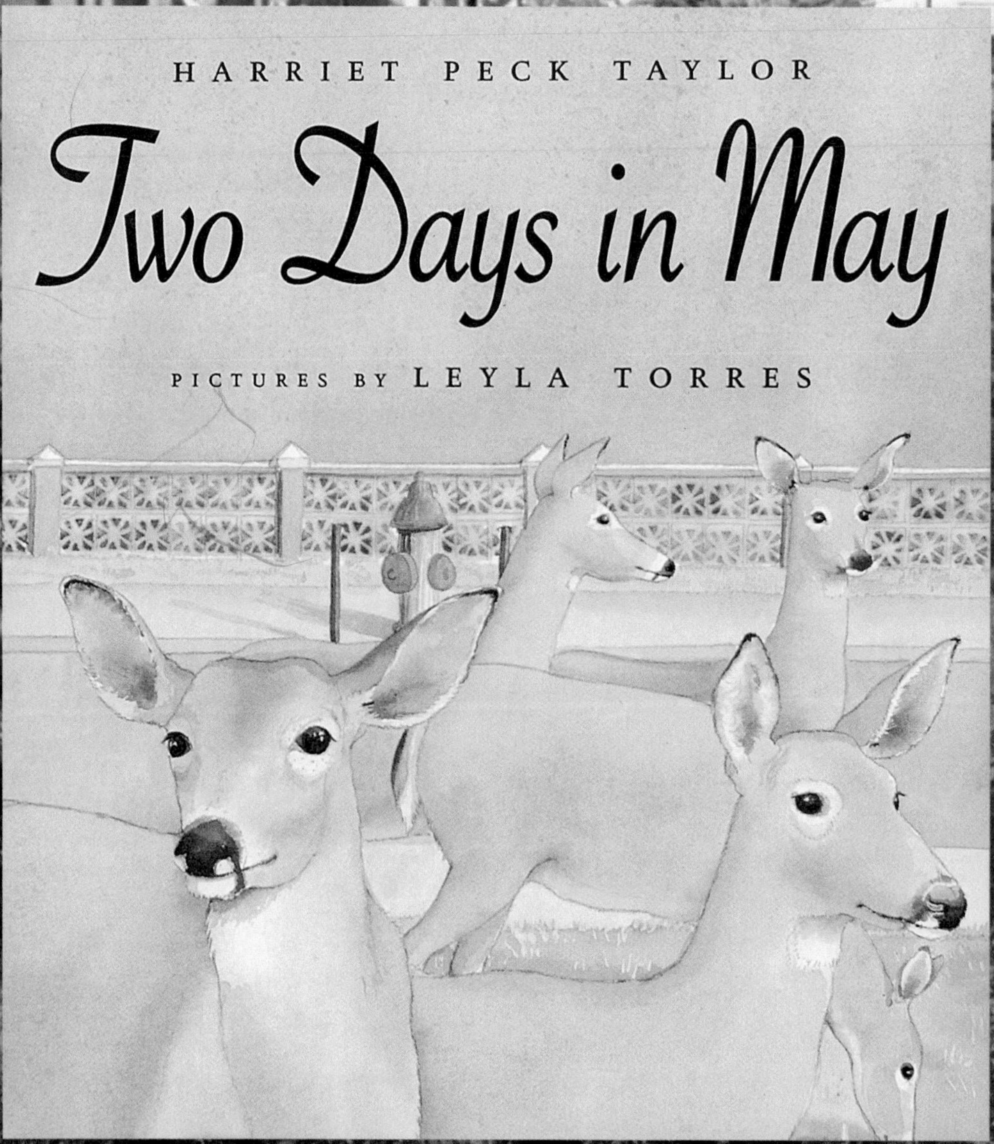
HARRIET PECK TAYLOR
Two Days in May
PICTURES BY LEYLA TORRES

Strategy Focus

As you read, pause to **monitor** how well you understand what happens in the story. **Clarify** any events that are confusing by rereading.

Early one Saturday morning in May, I went to our fire escape window and rubbed the sleep from my eyes. I looked down at the small garden I had planted behind our apartment building. Five animals were grazing on the new lettuce in my garden!

"Mama! Mama!" I called. "Come see what's in our yard!"

Mama hurried over to the window and gasped. "Sonia, those animals are deer, but how did they get here?" she asked. "I'll run and tell Mr. Donovan."

By the time Papa and I got out to the courtyard, a small crowd was gathering.

"Papa, why are there deer in the city?" I asked.

"The deer may have come all this way looking for food. They probably smelled your garden," he explained.

I thought I had never seen such an amazing sight. Their fur was a golden brown, and they balanced on tiny hooves. They had nervous tails, and eyes that were big and black and gentle.

Down the block a train rumbled by, but here life seemed to stand still. Pigeons and squirrels were almost the only birds or animals we ever saw in our neighborhood.

Looking around, I recognized many neighbors. There was Isidro Sánchez and his sister, Ana. Standing near me were Mr. Smiley, owner of Smiley's Laundromat, and my best friend, Peach, and Chester and Clarence Martin and the Yasamura sisters from down the hall. I saw Mr. Benny, the taxi driver, and the old Pigeon Lady, who was smiling brightly. I noticed that even neighbors who were almost strangers were standing close to each other and whispering in a friendly way. Well, everyone except Mr. Smiley and the Pigeon Lady, who were not on speaking terms. Mr. Smiley was angry because the Pigeon Lady fed her pigeons in front of his Laundromat, and he thought that was bad for business.

Mr. Donovan, our landlord, approached Papa. They spoke in hushed voices, but I was all ears.

"Luis, I, too, think the deer are really beautiful, but we both know they can't stay here," whispered Mr. Donovan. "They could be hit by a car. They belong in the woods, not in the city. I think we'd better call the animal control officers."

Papa nodded solemnly, and they walked off.

The Pigeon Lady came up to Peach and me and said, "Oh, girls, aren't they wonderful!"

"Yes!" we both answered together.

"I think two of the deer may be smaller. Those are probably females, or does. The males are called bucks. I used to see deer many years ago when I lived in the country."

Soon, Papa and Mr. Donovan returned with worried looks on their faces. They gathered the group together.

"The animal control office wants to shoot the deer," said Papa. "It's the law. The city is afraid the deer will starve."

"There aren't enough woods left for all the deer to find a home," added Mr. Donovan. "That's why the young deer wander far away. They're looking for territory of their own."

Everyone was so quiet that all you could hear were street sounds: honking and beeping, rumbling and humming.

Mr. Benny was the first to speak. "We can't let them shoot the deer. There must be another way."

"Yeah. That's right!" said Teresa Yasamura. All around, people were nodding in agreement.

Then Chester spoke up. "They wouldn't shoot the deer in front of this many people. It would be too dangerous."

"It's true!" exclaimed Papa. "We can form a human wall around the deer without getting too close."

"Right on!" said Isidro. "We'll stay here until we can figure out what to do."

And that was the beginning of our peaceful protest.

Mr. Benny wrinkled his brow. "I remember reading a few months back about an organization that rescues and relocates animals that are stranded or injured. A fox had been hit by a car but wasn't badly hurt. This outfit took it in until it healed and then found a new home for it far from busy streets. I'll go see if I can find the number."

A little while later, Mr. Benny returned and announced, "The wildlife rescuer isn't in at the moment, but I left a message for him to call. I said it was an emergency."

When the animal control officer arrived, he saw the crowd surrounding the deer and decided not to take any chances. "If you don't mind, folks," he said, "I'll just hang around until you've all had enough and gone home." But we weren't leaving.

We stayed all afternoon, waiting anxiously, hoping to hear from the rescue organization. We got to know one another better, and we learned more about the deer.

Peach's eyes were wide and bright. "Look how they rotate their big soft ears to the left and right," she exclaimed.

Clarence said, "We studied deer in science. Their hearing is very sharp. It helps them detect enemies approaching from far away."

Mr. Benny nodded as he walked over to us. "I sometimes see this kind of deer at night, in the headlights, when I drive way past the city limits. When they're startled by the taxi's lights, their tails go up like flags. The tails are white underneath, which means the animals are white-tailed deer."

The deer grazed and slept cautiously, always alert to danger. They watched us with curious, intelligent eyes. I could see that the people made them uncomfortable, and it helped me appreciate that these really were wild animals. We tried to keep our distance and not make any sudden movements.

When evening came, the crowd grew. We talked quietly and told jokes as we kept watch over our silent friends. We ordered pizza from Giuseppe's.

Ana Sánchez spoke to the animal control officer. "Would you like a slice of pizza?" she asked.

"Thanks so much," he said. "My name is Steve Scully, and I understand how hard this must be for all of you. This is the part of my job I dislike.

"The problem is population growth. We've built towns and highways where there were once forests and streams. Now there is very little habitat left for the deer. There is no easy solution." He shook his head sadly.

I begged Papa to let me sleep outside all night, since almost everyone was staying. Mama came out with my baby brother, Danny. She brought blankets, a quilt, a jacket, and even my stuffed dog, Hershey.

Mama sat close and draped her arm across my shoulders. "Are you sure you'll be warm enough, Sonia?" she asked.

"I'm sure," I said.

We sat silently together, admiring the deer.

Finally she said, "I have to go put Danny to bed." She kissed me on the top of my head. "Sweet dreams, pumpkin."

I slept like a bear cub, curled in a ball against Papa's broad back.

Next morning, I awoke with the sun in my eyes and city sounds buzzing in my ears. Papa hugged me and asked how I liked camping out.

"I dreamed I was sleeping with the deer in cool forests under tall trees."

"You were, Sonia!" he said, laughing. "But not in the forest."

I looked at the deer. "Has the wildlife rescuer called back?" I asked.

"Yes, Sonia. The organization called late last night and hopes to get someone out here this morning."

The group was quiet as we all continued to wait.

Later that morning, a rusty orange truck pulled up. The man who got out had a friendly, open face. All eyes were on him.

"Hi, folks. My name is Carl Jackson, and I'm with the wildlife rescue organization," he said. "I need to put the deer in crates in order to take them to our center. Don't be alarmed — I'm going to shoot them with a small amount of tranquilizer to make them sleep for a little while." Then, as they wobbled on unsteady legs, he grabbed them gently and guided them toward the wooden crates.

Carl turned to the crowd and smiled. "I'm an animal lover, too, and all of you should feel proud for helping save these deer. I'll find a home for them in the woods, where they'll be safe and happy and have plenty to eat."

Steve Scully came forward and extended his hand to Carl. "Glad you came, man."

A cheer went up from the crowd. People slapped each other on the back. Isidro high-fived everyone, including Mr. Donovan and the Pigeon Lady. Peach and I hugged each other, and Papa shook hands with Carl and Steve. I said good-bye to Teresa and Sandy Yasamura and to Mr. Benny.

I even saw Mr. Smiley shake the Pigeon Lady's hand. "Maybe you can feed the pigeons *behind* my Laundromat," he said. "I have a little space back there."

The Pigeon Lady smiled.

A few days later, Papa got a call from Carl. One of the does had given birth to two fawns! And Carl had found a home for all seven deer in a wooded area northwest of the city.

Sometimes, when I'm sitting on the fire escape, watching the flickering city lights, I think of the deer. In my mind, they're gliding silently across tall grass meadows all aglow in silver moonlight.

Where she was born: Lake Forest, Illinois

Where she lives now: Boulder, Colorado

Her animals: Taylor has lived with dogs, hamsters, lizards, a cat, a skunk named Stinky, and even a chinchilla.

Her books: When Taylor illustrates her own books, she creates batik designs using hot wax and colorful dyes.

Other books: *Coyote and the Laughing Butterflies, Ulaq and the Northern Lights*

Meet the Illustrator
Leyla Torres

Where she was born: Bogotá, Colombia

Where she lives now: New York City

Her first job: Making puppets

Her books: Torres visited children's libraries to learn more about art. These visits helped her decide to create her own books.

Other books: *Saturday Sancocho (El Sancocho del Sábado), Subway Sparrow (Gorrión del Metro)*

Internet

Wander through Education Place and discover more about these two author-illustrators.
www.eduplace.com/kids

Think About the Selection

1. Why doesn't Sonia get angry when the deer eat the lettuce in her garden?

2. Describe how Sonia's community works together to help save the deer.

3. Who do you think is the hero in this story? Give reasons for your answer.

4. How does Sonia's community change because of the two days the deer are in the neighborhood garden?

5. What animals do you see most often where you live? How do they behave when they are near people?

6. **Connecting/Comparing** Compare Sonia to another character in this theme.

Informing

Write a Newspaper Article

Tell others about the deer in the city. Write a newspaper article that explains how Sonia's community helped save the deer. Make sure your article includes who, what, where, when, and why. Write a headline at the top of your article.

Tips

- Look at a local newspaper for ideas.
- Write the most important information first.
- Use short, clear sentences.

Health

List Wildlife Safety Rules

In a small group, write a list of safety rules for people who come across wild animals. Create rules that will protect both the animal and the person. Look in the story and in other books or magazines for ideas.

Listening and Speaking

Role-Play Leaving a Phone Message

With a partner, practice leaving a phone message for a wildlife rescuer. Tell about the deer in the story, or choose another animal you might find where you live. Explain the problem and ask for help. If possible, tape-record your message and listen to how it sounds.

> **Tips**
> - Keep your message short.
> - Tell important details quickly and clearly.
> - Say "please" and "thank you."

Internet

Solve a Web Mystery Grid

Sometimes it leaps, sometimes it sleeps, and sometimes it does whatever it wants to. To discover what IT is, print out a mystery grid from Education Place. **www.eduplace.com/kids**

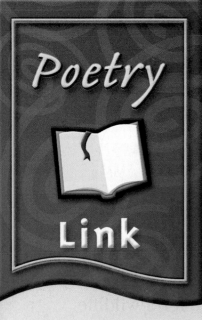
Skill: How to Read a Poem Aloud

❶ **Practice** reading the poem in a clear voice.

❷ **Change** the sound of your voice to help express the idea of the poem.

❸ **Pause** a little at the end of each line. **Pause longer** at punctuation marks.

❹ **Look** up at your listeners whenever you can.

January Deer

I am a January deer,
so swift and light
the hardpacked snow does not even
    crunch
beneath my hooves.
While others around me
sleep in silent caves,
    I run
through the white world
    with wide-open eyes.

Marilyn Singer

Seal

See how he dives
    From the rocks with a zoom!
See how he darts
    Through his watery room
    Past crabs and eels
        And green seaweed,
        Past fluffs of sandy
        Minnow feed!
    See how he swims
        With a swerve and a twist,
    A flip of the flipper,
    A flick of the wrist!
Quicksilver-quick,
Softer than spray,
Down he plunges
And sweeps away;
Before you can think,
Before you can utter
Words like "Dill pickle"
Or "Apple butter,"
Back up he swims
    Past Sting Ray and Shark,
    Out with a zoom,
    A whoop, a bark;
        Before you can say
        Whatever you wish,
        He plops at your side
        With a mouthful of fish!

William Jay Smith

97

Puffin-Stuff

See the little puffin,
Living by the sea,
Diving through the billows,
Catching fish for tea.

Dozing in the sunshine,
Nesting in the rocks,
Feather black tuxedo,
Little orange socks.

Joan Peronto

The Puffin

Upon this cake of ice is perched
The paddle-footed Puffin;
To find his double we have searched,
But have discovered — Nuffin!

Robert Williams Wood

Under the Trees

We scuffed through the woods
and didn't see anything,
anything big or small,

Didn't see a swallow
or a cottontail to follow
or a scamper or a whisk at all.

We *sat* in the woods
as quiet as anything,
quiet and tucked away,

And out came a rabbit
in his hoppy sort of habit,
and a chipmunk,
    and a robin,
        and a jay.

Aileen Fisher

Check Your Progress

You have just read about the habitats of puffins, seals, and deer. Now you will read two more selections about another habitat and compare these selections with the rest of the theme.

Think about the habitats that Bruce McMillan wrote about on pages 12–14. In what way does his message help you better understand the animals you've read about so far?

The next two selections are about the desert. One is fiction, and the other is nonfiction. As you read, think about how all the animal habitats in this theme are alike and different.

Read and Compare

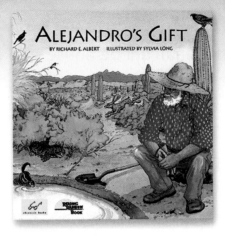

When Alejandro helps the desert animals, he also helps himself.

Try these strategies:
Predict and Infer
Monitor and Clarify

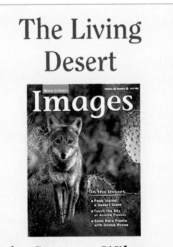

How do some desert animals survive the heat?

Try these strategies:
Summarize
Question

Strategies in Action *Be sure to use all of your reading strategies while you read.*

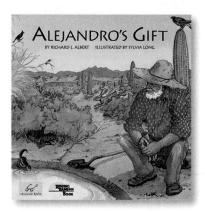

ALEJANDRO'S GIFT

BY RICHARD E. ALBERT
ILLUSTRATED BY SYLVIA LONG

Alejandro's small adobe house stood beside a lonely desert road.

Beside the house stood a well, and a windmill to pump water from the well. Water for Alejandro and for his only companion, a burro.

It was a lonely place, and Alejandro welcomed any who stopped by to refresh themselves at the well. But visitors were few, and after they left, Alejandro felt lonelier than before.

To more easily endure the lonely hours, Alejandro planted a garden. A garden filled with carrots, beans, and large brown onions.

Tomatoes and corn.

Melons, squash, and small red peppers.

Most mornings found Alejandro tending the garden, watching it grow. These were times he cherished, and he often stayed for hours, working until driven indoors by the desert heat.

The days went by, one after another with little change, until one morning when there was an unexpected visitor. This visitor came not from the desert road, but from the desert itself.

A ground squirrel crept from the underbrush. Moving warily over the sand, it hesitated and looked around. Alejandro paused, keeping very quiet as the squirrel approached the garden. It ran up to one of the furrows, drank its fill of water, and scampered away. After it left, Alejandro realized that for those few moments his loneliness had been all but forgotten.

And because he felt less lonely, Alejandro found himself hoping the squirrel would come again.

The squirrel did come again, from time to time bringing along small friends.

Wood rats and pocket gophers.

Jackrabbits, kangaroo rats, pocket mice.

Birds, too, became aware of Alejandro's garden.

Roadrunners, Gila woodpeckers, thrashers.

Cactus wrens, sage sparrows, mourning doves, and others came in the evening to perch on the branches of a mesquite bush, or to rest on the arms of a lone saguaro, before dropping down for a quick drink before nightfall.

Occasionally, even an old desert tortoise could be seen plodding toward the garden.

Suddenly, Alejandro found that time was passing more quickly. He was rarely lonely. He had only to look up from his hoe, or from wherever he might be at any moment, to find a small friend nearby.

For a while this was all that mattered to Alejandro, but after a time he wasn't so sure. He began asking himself if there was something more important than just making himself less lonely. It took Alejandro little time to see there was.

He began to realize that his tiny desert friends came to his garden not for company, but for water. And he found himself thinking of the other animals in the desert.

Animals like the coyote and the desert gray fox.

The bobcats, the skunks, the badgers, the long-nosed coatis.

The peccaries, sometimes called *javelinas*, the short-tempered wild pigs of the desert.

The antlered mule deer, the does, and the fawns.

Finding enough water was not a problem. With his windmill and well, Alejandro could supply ample water for any and all. Getting it to those who needed it was something else.

The something else, Alejandro decided, was a desert water hole.

Without delay, Alejandro started digging. It was tiring work, taking many days in the hot desert sun. But the thought of giving water to so many thirsty desert dwellers more than made up for the drudgery. And when it was filled, Alejandro was pleased with the gift he had made for his desert friends.

There was good reason to suppose it would take time for the larger animals to discover their new source of water, so Alejandro was patient. He went about as usual, feeding his burro, tending the garden, and doing countless other chores.

Days passed and nothing happened. Still, Alejandro was confident. But the days turned to weeks, and it was still quiet at the water hole. Why, Alejandro wondered, weren't they coming? What could he have done wrong?

The absence of the desert folk might have remained a mystery had Alejandro not come out of the house one morning when a skunk was in the clearing beyond the water hole. Seeing Alejandro, the skunk darted to safety in the underbrush.

It suddenly became very clear why Alejandro's gift was being shunned.

Alejandro couldn't believe he had been so thoughtless, but what was important now was to put things right as quickly as possible.

Water hole number two was built far from the house and screened by heavy desert growth. When it was filled and ready, Alejandro waited with mixed emotions. He was hopeful, yet he couldn't forget what had happened the first time.

As it turned out, he was not disappointed.

The animals of the desert did come, each as it made its own discovery. Because the water hole was now sheltered from the small adobe house and the desert road, the animals were no longer fearful. And although Alejandro could not see through the desert growth surrounding the water hole, he had ways of knowing it was no longer being shunned.

By the twitter of birds gathering in the dusk.

By the rustling of mesquite in the quiet desert evening telling of the approach of a coyote, a badger, or maybe a desert fox.

By the soft hoofbeats of a mule deer, or the unmistakable sound of a herd of peccaries charging toward the water hole.

And in these moments when Alejandro sat quietly listening to the sounds of his desert neighbors, he knew that the gift was not so much a gift that he had given, but a gift he had received.

Images

THE LIVING DESERT

by Suzanne Wilson

Desert animals live in blazing heat with very little water. How are they able to survive? Many animals use the giant saguaro cactus, which can store rainwater through its roots. Other animals rely on their own bodies and living habits to survive in the desert.

Think of the saguaro cactus as an apartment building and restaurant, an environment that feeds and houses many desert creatures. Birds and bats sip nectar from its flowers, and its fruit is eaten by rats, insects, and humans.

In spring, Gila woodpeckers peck out holes for nests. A hard lining forms inside, and moisture stored in the cactus keeps nests cool. The woodpeckers make new nests each year, and the empty holes gain new tenants. These include elf owls (the world's smallest owl, five inches long), cactus wrens, wood rats, and lizards. This handy housing is available for a long while, since a saguaro may live 200 years.

The saguaro, a small world in itself, has nectar for ▶ a cactus wren and a home for a tiny elf owl.

Large ears help a kit fox cool off, ▶ and long front legs are good for digging cool burrows.

Some animals carry their own air conditioning with them, attached to their heads! Their extra-large ears keep them cool. For example, the jack rabbit and the kit fox have much larger ears than do rabbits and foxes that live in cooler climates. Fine blood vessels near the surface of the ear carry heat away.

An animal's behavior helps it beat the heat, too. On summer days, the air temperature may reach 130°F, but nights cool down. The kit fox hunts rodents, rabbits, and ground-nesting birds at night. By day, it rests in an underground den. Many animals seek shelter underground during the day, when the sun-scorched surface may be 150°F. The temperature a foot below can be 65°F cooler.

Finally there are those creatures that actually seek the sun. Lizards need to bask in the heat to warm up their bodies enough to become active. Then they can move easily and hunt their prey.

The desert is full of wonders, each one different from the others. Whether plant or animal, each of these marvelous living things can cope with nature in its own way.

A yellow-headed, green-collared ▶ lizard begins its day by warming itself in the desert sunshine.

Think and Compare

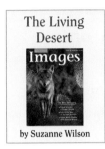

The Living Desert Images
by Suzanne Wilson

1. Compare the way Alejandro helps the animals with the way the animals help themselves in the "The Living Desert."

2. Both Alejandro and Ben want to be friends with the animals they meet. Are their reasons alike or different? Explain your answer.

3. Do you think people should be responsible for helping animals? Give examples from the selections or your own experiences.

4. How do the selections in this theme show how animals depend on their habitats?

Strategies in Action Tell about two or three places in *Alejandro's Gift* where you used reading strategies.

Write a Nature Log Entry

Suppose you are a scientist observing an animal in its habitat. Write a description of the animal's behavior in your log or notebook.

Tips

- Write the time of the observation, such as 9:15 A.M.
- Include some details about the animal's movement, sounds, and appearance.

✔ Vocabulary Items

Some test items ask you to identify a **synonym,** or a word that has almost the same meaning as another word. You need to decide which answer choice is the best one. A test on *Alejandro's Gift* might have this kind of test item.

Fill in the circle next to the best answer for the test item below.

1 Read this sentence from *Alejandro's Gift.* "Seeing Alejandro, the skunk <u>darted</u> to safety in the underbrush." Which word means about the same as *darted*?

   ○ swam   ○ walked   ○ fell   ● raced

---

 1 **Understand the question.**

Find the word that the question asks about. Is it shown in context? Decide what you need to do.

> This question asks about *darted.*
> The context of the sentence might
> help me. I need to choose the answer
> that means the same as *darted.*

② Think about what the word means.

Think about the word's parts. Look for the base word and prefix or suffix. How is the word used in the context?

If I take away the *-ed* ending, I see that the base word is *dart.* The context tells me that the skunk is moving fast because it's trying to escape.

③ Narrow the choices. Then choose the best answer.

Try each choice in the sentence. Which choices are clearly wrong? Have a reason for choosing the best answer. Guess only if you have to.

The story takes place in the desert, so *swam* is wrong. *Walked* sounds good, but it doesn't make sense in the sentence. *Fell* also doesn't make sense. I think the answer is *raced.*

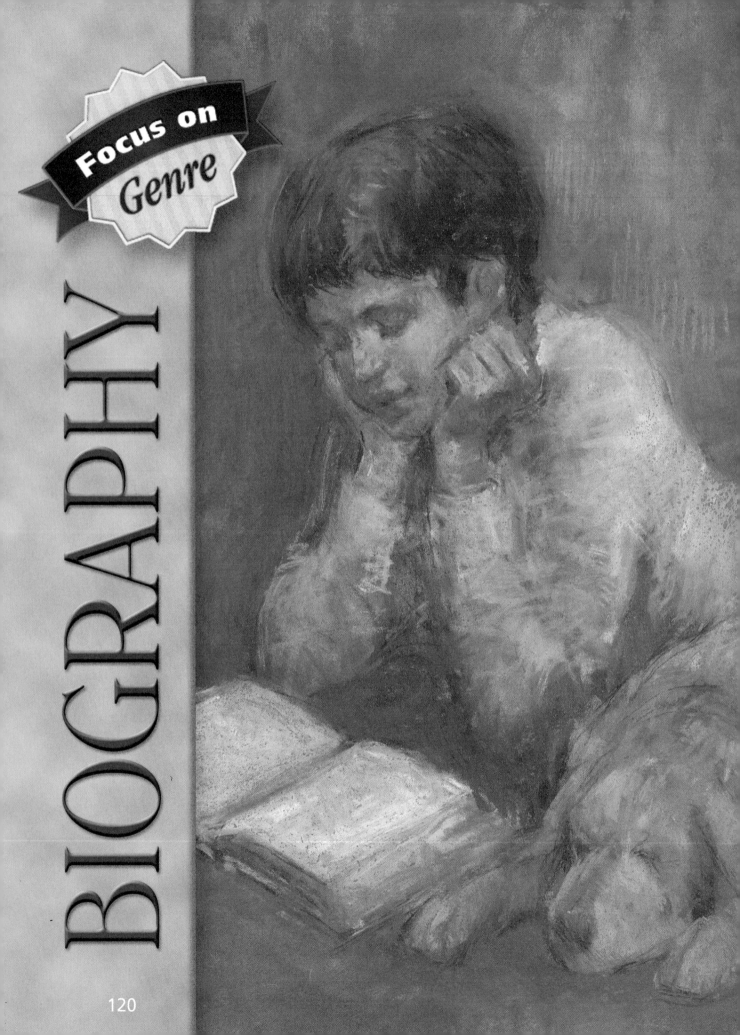

BIOGRAPHY

Biography

You can only live one life, but you can read about many others! A **biography** is a person's true life story. It gives facts and information about a person, often from the early years to the later years.

Here are four people you can learn about through their biographies.

CONTENTS

Focus on Genre

BECOMING A CHAMPION

The Babe Didrikson Story

by Stephen Berman

BABE DIDRIKSON once announced that she wanted to be "the greatest athlete that ever lived." She didn't say "woman athlete." She didn't think that way, and she didn't want others to think that way either. Whenever she had the chance, she competed with boys and men. And she beat them too!

Didrikson was born in Port Arthur, Texas, in 1911. Her parents named her Mildred. She was athletic and competitive. She always played just as hard as the boys, if not harder. One day she hit five home runs in a neighborhood baseball game. That day, the players nicknamed her "Babe," after the great baseball star Babe Ruth. The nickname stayed with her for life.

Babe wasn't just good at baseball, though. Basketball, tennis, track, diving — even bowling — came easily to her. And she said she loved them all. "I sleep them, eat them, talk them, and try my level best to do them as they should be done," she said.

In high school, Babe was a basketball star. In 1930, the owner of a Dallas insurance company saw her play. He offered her a job. With the job came the chance to star on the company's basketball team, the Golden Cyclones.

Babe practices for a basketball game, January, 1933.

As a Cyclone, Babe often scored thirty or more points a game. She led the team to the national women's basketball championships in 1930 and 1931. Other companies offered her higher pay, but Babe's company was starting a women's track-and-field team. She couldn't wait to try this new sport.

Once again, Babe excelled at something new. She was good at all three kinds of track-and-field events — running, jumping, and throwing. She decided to try out for the Olympics.

Babe jumps a hurdle.

1911

Born on June 26 in Port Arthur, Texas.

1930 – 1931

Joined the Golden Cyclones. Chosen as an All-American basketball player two years in a row.

1932

Won two gold medals (javelin and 80-meter hurdles) and a silver medal (high jump) at the Olympic Games in Los Angeles, California.

"I trained and trained and trained," she wrote to a friend. "I've been that way in every sport I've ever taken up." At the Olympic tryouts, she won five events and broke four world records. People called it the most amazing performance in track-and-field history — not just for a woman, but for anyone. Of course, she made the team too. And at the 1932 Olympic Games, Babe won three medals in track-and-field — one for every event she entered. At the end of the Olympics, she was as famous as Charles Lindbergh and Amelia Earhart.

Babe wasn't ready to rest, though. As a new challenge, she turned to golf. It turned out to be the greatest love of her life. She began practicing golf for up to sixteen hours a day. When her hands got sore and bruised from holding the clubs, she bandaged them and kept on playing.

Here's Babe warming up for the javelin throw.

1935

Began playing golf; went on to win 65 tournaments.

1945 – 1947

Chosen "Woman Athlete of the Year" by the Associated Press three years in a row.

1948

Won first U.S. Open golf tournament.

Babe's humor and self-confidence brought her attention and friends wherever she went. Even male golfers had to laugh when she announced, "OK, now Babe's here! Now who's gonna finish second?"

Golf made Babe famous and wealthy. But she cared about more than her own success. She was also determined to help others succeed. Babe helped start the Ladies Professional Golf Association so that other women could pursue a career in golf. And her own powerful example showed others that women could and should be involved in sports.

Babe loved to entertain her fans with jokes and trick shots.

1949

Helped start the Ladies Professional Golf Association.

1950

Chosen "Woman Athlete of the Year" and "Woman Athlete of the Half Century" by the Associated Press. Won second U.S. Open golf tournament.

Babe earned many honors. She won titles in basketball, track, and golf. She was named Woman Athlete of the Year six times. In 1950, sportswriters named her the greatest female athlete for the years 1900–1950. Babe decided she wanted to be the greatest in the next fifty years too.

Then in 1953, she became ill with cancer. Doctors told her she would never play golf again. They were wrong. "Babe was a very brave girl or she could never have become the person she was," a friend once said. Babe's bravery took her back to first place in less than a year.

Two years later, in 1956, Babe died. Finally, cancer was the one thing she couldn't beat. But she was a fierce competitor until the very end.

Babe signed autographs for fans of all ages.

1954

Chosen "Woman Athlete of the Year" by the Associated Press. Won third U.S. Open golf tournament.

1956

Died on September 26 in Galveston, Texas.

1999

Chosen as one of the top ten "Athletes of the Century" by ESPN.

Focus on **Genre**

Bill Meléndez

An Artist in Motion

by Stephen Berman

Bill Meléndez

Bill Meléndez wasn't born with a crayon in his hand, but it wasn't long before he picked one up. As a boy, he doodled on every scrap of paper he could find. As an adult, he turned his love of drawing into his career. Today, he is one of the world's most successful animators.

Meléndez was born in Mexico in 1916. His parents named him José. When his family moved to the United States, everyone began calling him Bill. Meléndez already spoke Spanish. In his new home, he quickly learned English as well. He went to high school and then to college in Los Angeles, California.

As a young man, Meléndez worked at all kinds of jobs. Then in 1938, he found his first job as an artist. The Walt Disney studios hired him to work as an animator. It was the perfect job for him. As an animator, Meléndez had to draw, draw, draw, all day long. And he loved it.

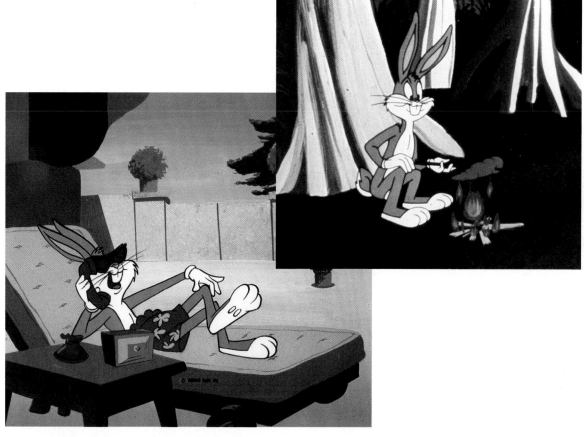

Meléndez has animated many famous cartoon characters, including Bugs Bunny.

An animator brings cartoon characters to life by making them appear to move. To show this movement, animators must create thousands of drawings. Each drawing is a little bit different from the one before it. These drawings show the beginning and ending of each movement, and all the steps in between.

Today, many animators use computers. But when Meléndez first started animating, every drawing had to be created by hand. Some people might think this sounds boring, but not Meléndez. "Animators don't think of it as drawing one drawing after another after another. We think of it as illustrating action," he says. The joy of his job, he explains, is that "with a light and fun touch, you can create the feeling that these are real people."

Meléndez soon began animating many famous cartoon characters, including Schroeder and Lucy from *Peanuts* (above).

Meléndez started working at Disney when Mickey Mouse cartoons were first becoming popular. Disney needed lots of animators — and fast. "They were hiring anybody who could draw a straight line!" Meléndez says. "Now, I had never really studied art, but in school I was always doodling. I was drawing, drawing, drawing, just for the fun of it, all the time. So, when I was hired by Disney I thought, 'What a fun job!'"

At Disney, Meléndez made Donald Duck and Mickey Mouse waddle and stroll across the screen. He made their beaks and mouths move so that they seemed to talk. He made Mickey hold his belly when he laughed. Meléndez also worked on the famous Disney animated movies *Pinocchio, Fantasia, Dumbo,* and *Bambi.*

In 1941, Meléndez went to work for a company called Warner Brothers. There he animated other well-known cartoon characters, such as Bugs Bunny, Daffy Duck, and Porky Pig.

But Meléndez may be most famous as the animator of the "Peanuts" characters — Snoopy, Charlie Brown, Lucy, and the rest of the gang. Meléndez first animated some of these characters for television commercials. Then he began working with the creator of "Peanuts," Charles Schulz, to make movies and TV specials, such as *A Charlie Brown Christmas*. He's even created some of the sound effects for the movies. "I do Snoopy's growls, grunts, and howls," he says. "AAOOOOOO! Recognize that howl?"

Meléndez started his own animation studio, Bill Meléndez Productions, in 1964. He likes working with other people much more than he likes drawing by himself. "I tried working at home — it just made me nervous!" he says. "At the studio there's a team of us, a whole bunch of people laughing over this and that, giving each other feedback. It makes work fun and easier."

Animation is always hard work. Still, Meléndez would never trade it for making movies and TV shows with real, live actors. "The best animation does what can't be done in live action," he says. "Nothing is impossible in animation. That's the magic of it!"

Meléndez helped bring the whole *Peanuts* gang to life.

BRAVE Bessie Coleman

Pioneer Aviator

by Veronica Freeman Ellis

On October 15, 1922, at an air show in Chicago, Illinois, all eyes were on the sky. A crowd watched a small stunt plane high above begin to dive at top speed. Would it crash? Suddenly, at the last minute, the plane swooped up, shot over the heads of the spectators, and climbed back up into the air. The crowd applauded and cheered!

Coleman with her first airplane, a Curtiss JN-4, also called a Jenny.

Flying the plane was Bessie Coleman, the first African American to earn a pilot's license. Two years before, Coleman had left Chicago to follow her dreams of flight. Airplanes were still new inventions. In 1903, the Wright brothers had flown the first powered airplane. By 1922, large audiences were flocking to air shows to enjoy the amazing sight of "barnstormers," stunt pilots who flew in loops and spins through the air. Coleman had returned to Chicago to show her family and friends that she, too, could soar across the sky like a bird.

A plane flying over the Chicago airfield during an air show in August, 1911.

Coleman looked brave when she waved to the crowd from the open cockpit of her plane. And she really looked brave when her plane flipped upside down, swirled in spirals, or plunged toward the ground and streaked back upward! But Coleman's bravest actions took place long before she ever learned to fly. During her lifetime, many people didn't believe that women could do something as difficult and dangerous as piloting a plane. African Americans like Coleman were not allowed to attend the same schools, work at the same jobs, or live in the same neighborhoods as white people. But Coleman refused to let these problems get in her way. She set the highest goals for herself and reached them — against enormous odds.

Coleman was born in 1892. She grew up in Waxahachie, Texas. While her mother worked as a maid, Coleman cared for her sisters, earned money by working in the cotton fields,

A plane performing an upside-down roll in the early 1920s.

and still found time to do her schoolwork. After high school, she went to Langston College in Oklahoma. She could only afford to attend classes for one year. But by that time, she had already set her sights on the sky.

Coleman discovered that in 1911, Harriet Quimby had become the first American woman to receive a pilot's license. Coleman was fascinated. She thought it must be wonderful to fly. After leaving college, Coleman moved to Chicago. There, as she looked in libraries and newspapers for more information, she decided that she wanted to go to flying school. However, few aviation schools in the United States were willing to train women. None of the schools would train an African American woman.

Coleman wrote many letters to set up her air shows. Her writing paper (above) showed some of her stunts.

Coleman remained determined. She decided to travel to France, where women and people of color had better opportunities. There, she attended one of the best aviation schools in the country. In 1921, she earned her pilot's license.

When Coleman returned to the United States, no one would hire her as a pilot because she was African American and a woman. To make a living, she became a barnstormer. Coleman was one of the most daring barnstormers of them all! Her thrilling stunts earned her the nicknames "Queen Bess" and "Brave Bessie."

Coleman used her talent to fight for her beliefs. She would not perform at air shows unless African Americans

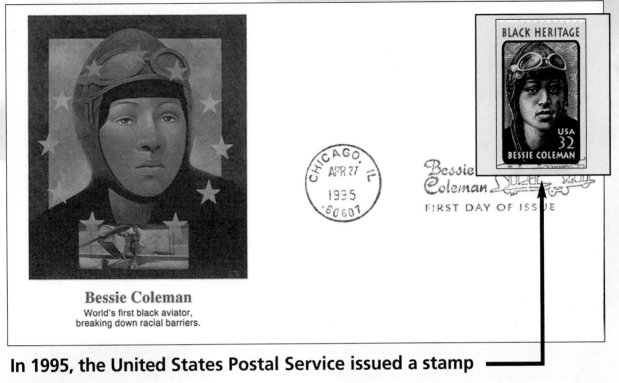

Bessie Coleman
World's first black aviator,
breaking down racial barriers.

BLACK HERITAGE

USA
32
BESSIE COLEMAN

Bessie Coleman
FIRST DAY OF ISSUE

In 1995, the United States Postal Service issued a stamp honoring Coleman.

were allowed to attend. In Waxahachie, she refused to fly until people of color were allowed to enter through the same gate as white people. She visited schools and churches all over the United States to encourage African Americans to follow their own dreams — and to learn to fly.

More than anything, Coleman wanted to start a school to train African American aviators. Sadly, on April 30, 1926, Coleman was rehearsing for an air show when the gears on her plane jammed. The plane spun out of control and crashed. Coleman died doing what she loved most. But her shining example will always live on: When you face obstacles, just fly right over them.

Focus on Genre

Hank Greenberg

All-Around All-Star

by Becky Cheston

Hank Greenberg

Hank Greenberg

First big league home run: May 6, 1933

American League MVP: 1935 and 1940

All-Star Team: 1938 and 1940

Elected to Hall of Fame: January 25, 1956

Going for the record: In 1938, Greenberg hit 58 home runs, almost beating Babe Ruth's record of 60.

It was July 1, 1945. It had been four years, one month, and twenty-four days since Hank Greenberg had last thrilled fans with a home run. Now, back from World War II, he was again up at bat. A cheering crowd waited to see what the star slugger for the Detroit Tigers would do.

Before the war, Greenberg had twice been voted the American League's Most Valuable Player. And in 1938, before Mark McGwire and Sammy Sosa were even born, Greenberg gave baseball fans a summer to remember when he almost wiped out Babe Ruth's home run record. But on that day in 1945, fans must have been wondering — did Greenberg still have what it takes to be an all-star? The answer was in his actions. Greenberg smacked a homer into the left-field seats.

The secret to Greenberg's success as a ball player was hard work and determination. Even when people said he was too tall, or called him names because he was Jewish, Greenberg always held on to his dream of playing in the big leagues. "I wasn't a natural ball player like Babe Ruth or Willie Mays, but if you practice the way I did — all day long, day after day — you're bound to get pretty good," Greenberg said.

Greenberg jumps high to catch a long fly ball during spring training for the Detroit Tigers.

As a child, Greenberg rushed home every day after school, grabbed his bat, glove, and ball, and dashed to the ballpark. To work on his hitting, he asked friends to pitch to him. To improve his fielding, he asked friends to hit the ball to him, while he counted how many he could catch in a row.

In 1929, Greenberg was invited to play baseball for several professional teams. He joined the Detroit Tigers. In 1930, he started training in the minor leagues. He spent three long years in the minors, watching, practicing, and learning.

Greenberg at the plate, ready to hit the ball for his team.

Finally, in 1933, Greenberg got his chance. In his first major league start with the Tigers, Greenberg smashed the ball out of the park — a home run!

Playing baseball wasn't always fun for Greenberg, though. Whenever he went up to bat, some of the fans and players would call him names because he was Jewish. But over time, as he led the Tigers to win four pennants and two World Series, he earned the respect of those around him.

In the last game of the 1945 season, Greenberg hit a grand-slam home run in the ninth inning. His homer won the American League pennant for the Detroit Tigers.

In the summer of 1934, Greenberg did something else that made people admire him. The Tigers were in a race to win the American League pennant. Every game mattered. But one game was scheduled on Yom Kippur, an important Jewish holiday. Greenberg decided not to play.

Everyone was talking about it. Edgar Guest, a famous poet, even wrote about Greenberg:

We shall miss him on the infield and shall miss him at the bat,
But he's true to his religion — and I honor him for that!

When Greenberg entered his synagogue that day, everyone applauded. Greenberg had become a hero.

Greenberg was also a good team player. In 1940, the Tigers had a new hitter. The only position on the field he could play was first base — Greenberg's job. The Tigers asked Greenberg to play in the outfield. Some players might have stormed off in anger, but not Greenberg. Instead, he agreed to switch. At first he had trouble playing left field. But he practiced long hours before and after games. He even got the peanut vendors and kids who hung around the ballpark to hit to him!

Greenberg (at right) was named to the All-Star team twice. Another famous first baseman, Lou Gehrig (at left), was on the team too.

During World War II, Greenberg was the first baseball star to join the Armed Forces. He left baseball, a job that paid him $11,000 a month, to earn $21 a month as a soldier. "My country comes first," Greenberg said. Once again, people admired Greenberg for more than his baseball talent.

In 1947, Greenberg retired from playing baseball, but he never really left the game behind. He worked as a team manager and an owner. In 1956, he received baseball's highest honor when he was elected to the Hall of Fame. He was the first Jewish player to be elected. Greenberg died on September 5, 1986. He will always be remembered as an all-star — both on and off the playing field.

Greenberg (left) with Joe DiMaggio, September 3, 1939.

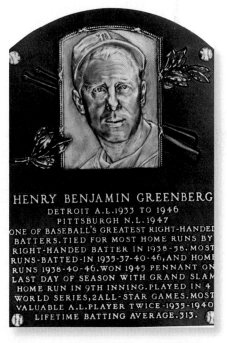

Greenberg's plaque at the National Baseball Hall of Fame in Cooperstown, New York.

Think About the
BIOGRAPHIES

1. Compare the problems that Bessie Coleman and Hank Greenberg have. How are they alike? How are they different?

2. Babe Didrikson chose a career in sports, and Bill Melendez chose a career in animation. Are those careers alike in any way? Explain why or why not.

3. Do you think meeting a challenge can make a difference in someone's life? Use examples from the selections.

4. Which person in these four biographies do you most admire? Why?

Internet

Post a Review

Which biography did you like best? Write a review of one of the biographies. Tell what you liked or did not like. Post your review on our Web site. **www.eduplace.com/kids**

146

Write a Biography

Find out more about a person you are curious about. The person could be a president, an explorer, or a musician. Look up facts about the person in books, in magazines, in the encyclopedia, or on the Internet. Write a biography of the person.

Tips

- Start the biography with an important event or a special fact about the person.
- In the main part of the biography, write about the person's early life first. Then tell about the person's later years.
- Write an exciting title that will get a reader's attention.

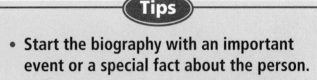

Martin Luther King, Jr.

Michelle Kwan

Louisa May Alcott

Neil Armstrong

148

5

Voyagers

Travellers

Come, let us go a-roaming!

The world is all our own,

And half its paths are still untrod,

And half its joys unknown.

from the poem
by Arthur St. John Adcock

Voyagers

with Sook Nyul Choi

Greetings Boys and Girls,

Welcome to Voyagers! In this theme, you'll see that voyagers all have one thing in common. They all have courage. Let me describe what I mean.

When I was a young girl growing up in Korea, I loved reading books about the United States. I wondered what it would be like to live there.

During high school, I made up my mind. I wanted to go to college in the United States. My brothers and sister told me that I would be lonely living in a new country. What if my brothers and sister were right? What if I never made any friends in America? I was really scared.

Whenever I got scared, my mother was there to help. She knew how much I wanted to go to the United States. My mother gave me courage by telling me that I would make new friends.

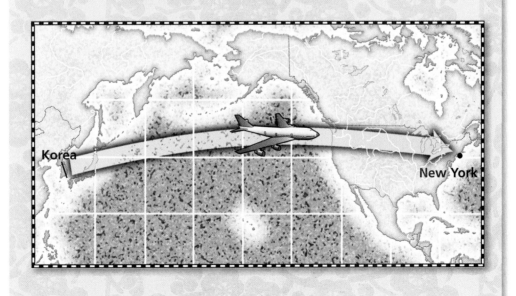

Korea

New York

Manhattanville College

Wow, was my mother right! I was never lonely, not even on the day I arrived. When I stepped out of the taxi at Manhattanville College in New York, my new roommate and her friends were waiting for me. They rushed over and hugged me. I was so surprised! In Korea, people bow when they greet each other. They don't hug. Best friends in Korea only hold hands. But I loved getting that big hug from my new friends. It was really special.

So you see, all you need to take a voyage is a little courage. Keep that in mind as you read about the voyagers in this theme.

With best wishes to
all young voyagers,

Sook Nyul Choi

During her first year at Manhattanville College, Sook Nyul Choi gave a speech to her class.

152

Take a Voyage

Think about the courage Sook Nyul Choi showed by coming to the United States. Was there ever a time in your life when you needed courage? What was that like? As you read the selections in this theme, look for ways the voyagers all show courage.

It's time to go! You'll travel on the *Mayflower*, walk across the South Pole, and discover Hawaii. By the end of this theme, you will all be voyagers!

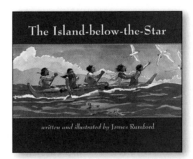

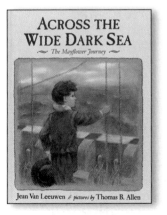

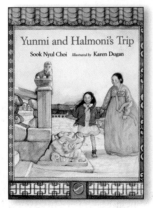

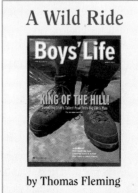

Internet

To learn about the authors in this theme, visit Education Place. **www.eduplace.com/kids**

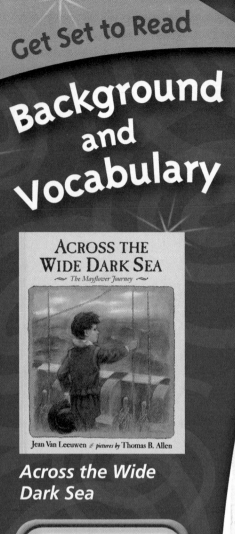

ACROSS THE
WIDE DARK SEA
~ The Mayflower Journey ~

Jean Van Leeuwen & pictures by Thomas B. Allen

**Across the Wide
Dark Sea**

Read to find
the meanings
of these words.

e Glossary

anchor

cramped

journey

seeping

settlement

survive

weary

Journey of the Pilgrims

It's hard to imagine making a long **journey** across stormy seas on a **cramped** and crowded ship. But in 1620, that's exactly what the Pilgrims did. They traveled all the way across the Atlantic Ocean from England to America on a ship called the *Mayflower*.

The sea was rough, and water was constantly **seeping** through the walls of the ship. After sixty-six days, the **weary** travelers reached America and dropped the ship's **anchor**. Only one Pilgrim did not **survive** the trip.

After exploring the area, the Pilgrims built a **settlement** and named it Plymouth. In *Across the Wide Dark Sea*, you will read about the incredible journey the Pilgrims made and their struggle to build a new home.

This cradle belonged to the family of Peregrine White, the first Pilgrim child born in America.

Mayflower II, a full-size version of what the first *Mayflower* may have looked like, now floats in Plymouth Harbor in Massachusetts.

A cooking pot was one of the most useful things families brought on the *Mayflower*. This one belonged to the Standish family.

MEET THE AUTHOR
Jean Van Leeuwen

MEET THE ILLUSTRATOR
Thomas B. Allen

For Jean Van Leeuwen, getting lost in a good book is great fun. As a child, she would get so interested in a book that when anyone called her name she would look up wondering where she was! Now Van Leeuwen writes books, too. Sometimes an idea just strikes her like lightning. As she says, "For me, each book begins with a thunderbolt from the sky."

Other books:

A Fourth of July on the Plains, Nothing Here But Trees, The Strange Adventures of Blue Dog

Thomas B. Allen likes to mix and match his tools when he draws. For this book he used charcoal, pastels, and colored pencils on rough, bumpy paper to give him just the look he wanted. Allen also illustrated *Going West,* another book by Jean Van Leeuwen.

Other books:

Climbing Kansas Mountains (by George Shannon)

Good-bye, Charles Lindbergh (by Louise Borden)

A Green Horn Blowing (by David F. Birchman)

Internet

Visit Education Place to discover more about Jean Van Leeuwen and Thomas B. Allen.
www.eduplace.com/kids

ACROSS THE WIDE DARK SEA
~ The Mayflower Journey ~

Jean Van Leeuwen & pictures by Thomas B. Allen

Strategy Focus

As you read this story of one boy's journey across the sea, think of **questions** about the Pilgrims and their struggle for survival.

I stood close to my father as the anchor was pulled dripping from the sea. Above us, white sails rose against a bright blue sky. They fluttered, then filled with wind. Our ship began to move.

My father was waving to friends on shore. I looked back at their faces growing smaller and smaller, and ahead at the wide dark sea. And I clung to my father's hand.

We were off on a journey to an unknown land.

The ship was packed tight with people — near a hundred, my father said. We were crowded below deck in a space so low that my father could barely stand upright, and so cramped that we could scarcely stretch out to sleep.

Packed in tight, too, was everything we would need in the new land: tools for building and planting, goods for trading, guns for hunting. Food, furniture, clothing, books. A few crates of chickens, two dogs, and a striped orange cat.

Our family was luckier than most. We had a corner out of the damp and cold. Some had to sleep in the ship's small work boat.

160

The first days were fair, with a stiff wind.

My mother and brother were seasick down below. But I stood on deck and watched the sailors hauling on ropes, climbing in the rigging, and perched at the very top of the mast, looking out to sea.

What a fine life it must be, I thought, to be a sailor.

One day clouds piled up in the sky. Birds with black wings circled the ship, and the choppy sea seemed angry.

"Storm's coming," I heard a sailor say. We were all sent below as the sailors raced to furl the sails.

Then the storm broke. Wind howled and waves crashed. The ship shuddered as it rose and fell in seas as high as mountains. Some people were crying, others praying. I huddled next to my father, afraid in the dark.

How could a ship so small and helpless ever cross the vast ocean?

The sun came out. We walked on deck and dried our clothes. But just when my shoes felt dry at last, more clouds gathered.

"Storm's coming," I told my father.

So the days passed, each one like the last. There was nothing to do but eat our meals of salt pork, beans, and bread, tidy up our cramped space, sleep when we could, and try to keep dry. When it was not too stormy, we climbed on deck to stretch our legs. But even then we had to keep out of the sailors' way.

How I longed to run and jump and climb!

Once during a storm a man was swept overboard. Reaching out with desperate hands, he caught hold of a rope and clung to it.

Down he went under the raging foaming water.

Then, miraculously, up he came.

Sailors rushed to the side of the ship. Hauling on the rope, they brought him in close and with a boat hook plucked him out of the sea. And his life was saved.

Storm followed storm. The pounding of wind and waves caused one of the main beams to crack, and our ship began to leak.

Worried, the men gathered in the captain's cabin to talk of what to do. Could our ship survive another storm? Or must we turn back?

They talked for two days, but could not agree.

Then someone thought of the iron jack for raising houses that they were taking to the new land. Using it to lift the cracked beam, the sailors set a new post underneath, tight and firm, and patched all the leaks.

And our ship sailed on.

For six weeks we had traveled, and still there was no land in sight. Now we were always cold and wet. Water seeping in from above put out my mother's cooking fire, and there was nothing to eat but hard dry biscuits and cheese. My brother was sick, and many others too.

And some began to ask why we had left our safe homes to go on this endless journey to an unknown land.

Why? I also asked the question of my father that night.

"We are searching for a place to live where we can worship God in our own way," he said quietly. "It is this freedom we seek in a new land. And I have faith that we will find it."

Looking at my father, so calm and sure, suddenly I too had faith that we would find it.

Still the wide dark sea went on and on. Eight weeks. Nine.

Then one day a sailor, sniffing the air, said, "Land's ahead." We dared not believe him. But soon bits of seaweed floated by. Then a tree branch. And a feather from a land bird.

Two days later at dawn I heard the lookout shout, "Land ho!"

Everyone who was well enough to stand crowded on deck. And there through the gray mist we saw it: a low dark outline between sea and sky. Land!

Tears streamed down my mother's face, yet she was smiling. Then everyone fell to their knees while my father said a prayer of thanksgiving.

Our long journey was over.

The ship dropped anchor in a quiet bay, circled by land. Pale yellow sand and dark hunched trees were all we saw. And all we heard was silence.

What lurked among those trees? Wild beasts? Wild men? Would there be food and water, a place to take shelter?

What waited for us in this new land?

A small party of men in a small boat set off to find out. All day I watched on deck for their return.

When at last they rowed into sight, they brought armfuls of firewood and tales of what they had seen: forests of fine trees, rolling hills of sand, swamps and ponds and rich black earth. But no houses or wild beasts or wild men.

So all of us went ashore.

My mother washed the clothes we had worn for weeks beside a shallow pond, while my brother and I raced up and down the beach.

We watched whales spouting in the sparkling blue bay and helped search for firewood. And we found clams and mussels, the first fresh food we had tasted in two months. I ate so many I was sick.

Day after day the small party set out from the ship, looking for just the right place to build our settlement.

The days grew cold. Snowflakes danced in the wind. The cold and damp made many sick again. Drawing his coat tightly around him, my father looked worried.

"We must find a place," he said, "before winter comes."

One afternoon the weary men returned with good news. They had found the right spot at last.

When my father saw it, he smiled. It was high on a hill, with a safe harbor and fields cleared for planting and brooks running with sweet water. We named it after the town from which we had sailed, across the sea.

It was December now, icy cold and stormy. The men went ashore to build houses, while the rest of us stayed on board ship. Every fine day they worked. But as the houses of our settlement began to rise, more and more of our people fell sick. And some of them died.

It was a long and terrible winter.

We had houses now, small and rough. Yet the storms and sickness went on. And outside the settlement, Indians waited, seldom seen but watching us.

My father and mother nursed the sick, and my father led prayers for them. But more and more died. Of all the people who had sailed for the new land, only half were left.

One morning in March, as I was gathering firewood, I heard a strange sweet sound. Looking up, I saw birds singing in a white birch tree.

Could it be that spring had come at last?

All that day the sun shone warm, melting the snow. The sick rose from their beds. And once more the sound of axes and the smell of new-split wood filled the air.

"We have done it," my father said. "We have survived the winter."

But now the Indians came closer. We found their arrows, and traces of their old houses. We caught sight of them among the trees. Our men met to talk of this new danger. How could so small a settlement defend itself?

Cannons were mounted on top of the hill, and the men took turns standing guard. Then one day an Indian walked into the settlement. Speaking to us in our own language, he said, "Welcome."

Our Indian friend came back and brought his chief. We all agreed to live in peace.

And one of the Indians stayed with us, teaching us where to find fish in the bubbling brooks, and how to catch them in traps, and how to plant Indian corn so that next winter we would have enough to eat.

My father and I worked side by side, clearing the fields, planting barley and peas and hills of corn.

Afterward I dug a garden next to our house. In it we planted the seeds we had brought from home: carrots and cabbages and onions and my mother's favorite herbs, parsley, sage, chamomile, and mint.

Each day I watched, until something green pushed up from the dark earth. My mother laughed when she saw it.

"Perhaps we may yet make a home in this new land," she said.

On a morning early in April our ship sailed back across the sea. We gathered on shore to watch it go. The great white sails filled with wind, then slowly the ship turned and headed out into the wide dark sea.

I watched it growing smaller and smaller, and suddenly there were tears in my eyes. We were all alone now.

Then I felt a hand on my shoulder.

"Look," my father said, pointing up the hill.

Spread out above us in the soft spring sunshine was our settlement: the fields sprouting with green, the thatch-roofed houses and neatly fenced gardens, the streets laid out almost like a town.

"Come," my father said. "We have work to do."

With his hand on my shoulder we walked back up the hill.

Responding

ACROSS THE WIDE DARK SEA
— The Mayflower Journey —

Jean Van Leeuwen ✧ pictures by Thomas B. Allen

Think About the Selection

1. Why do the people in this story travel to an unknown land? In what ways do they hope their lives will be different?

2. How do you think the boy's feelings about a sailor's life change during the voyage?

3. Why do you think the settlers name their new town after the one they sailed from?

4. What would you find most difficult and most exciting about the voyage the boy makes?

5. What tools and machines that we have today would have been most useful to the settlers?

6. **Connecting/Comparing** What qualities do the settlers have that help them succeed on their voyage?

Summarizing

Write a Travel Diary

Choose one part of the story, such as the voyage, the first winter in the new land, or the first spring. Write an entry for a travel diary that summarizes the important events during that time.

Tips

- To get started, brainstorm a list of events or make a story web.
- Include descriptive details.
- Keep your summary short.

Math

Calculate Amounts

If a person on the *Mayflower* ate one pound of salt pork, one cup of beans, half a pound of cheese, and three biscuits each day, how much of each of those foods would a person eat in one week? Try drawing a picture to help you find the answer.

Bonus **The journey lasted sixty-six days. How much would one traveler have eaten during the entire trip?**

Vocabulary

Make a Picture Dictionary

With a partner, write all the words from the story about ships and sailing on separate pieces of paper. Look up each word in a dictionary, write down its meaning, and draw a picture of it. Staple your pages together in alphabetical order to make a book.

Internet

Build a Model of the Mayflower

Find instructions on how to build your own paper sailing ship when you connect to Education Place. **www.eduplace.com/kids**

Young Voyagers
A Pilgrim Childhood

What was life like for the twenty-eight children aboard the *Mayflower*? How did they live once they settled in America? Read on to find out.

On Board the Mayflower

The *Mayflower* was built to carry cargo, not people. Passengers lived in the lower decks — the dark, cramped space between the hold and the main deck.

The *Mayflower II*, shown here, has a staircase between decks. The first *Mayflower* had only a ladder.

In good weather, children might have read, played games, or exercised on deck. Much of the time, however, the passengers had to stay below deck because of stormy weather. They were often seasick, and the ship's motion — up and down, side to side — made their cramped living space dangerous.

The voyage was filled with hardships, but there were joyful events as well. One baby was born during the voyage and named Oceanus. (Can you guess why his parents gave him that name?) Another child, Peregrine White, was born in Cape Cod Harbor. His first name means "traveler."

After sixty-six days at sea, the Pilgrims were happy and relieved to finally reach their new home.

Parts of the Ship

A. The **Round House** was where the ship's route was planned, using maps and other charts.

B. The **Ship's Bell** was rung during emergencies or to show the passage of time.

C. The **Great Cabin** was where the commander of the ship lived.

D. The **Whipstaff** was a long lever used to steer the ship.

E. The **Cook-room** was where meals were prepared for the crew.

F. The **lower decks** were where the passengers lived.

G. The **Hold** was where most of the food, tools, and supplies were kept.

Living in New Plymouth

What was life like in Plymouth? At Plimoth Plantation in Massachusetts, where these photos were taken, people dress up and show visitors what Pilgrim life may have been like. The facts may surprise you!

Children spent most of the day working! Their chores included fetching water, gathering firewood, herding animals, and gathering berries. They also helped their parents cook, clean, plant and harvest crops, and care for younger children.

Children and adults probably took baths only a few times a year. They thought bathing was unhealthy.

Pilgrim children still had time to play. They probably played marbles, ball games, board games, and running games.

At seven years old, children began dressing like their parents. Before that, both boys and girls wore gowns.

There was no school in the early years of New Plymouth. Children learned to read and write from their parents or from neighbors.

Older children were expected to serve meals to their parents. Children ate only after their parents had been served. They often ate while standing at the table.

A Description

A description is a picture in words that helps the reader. Use this student's writing as a model when you write a description of your own.

A Trip I Have Taken

I love going on trips. It was the end of summer, and my family was planning to go on a picnic. I was very excited because picnics are fun and I get to see a lot of interesting things on our way to the park.

It was a rainy day, and the highway looked all smoky as the cars went swishing by. At times the cars beside us splashed water on our car, and I would dodge for cover, not remembering that the water could not come inside. We kept hoping there would be sun where the picnic was.

It was a very busy highway with a lot of big trucks. I am scared of the trucks, especially when they have to blow their horns. It reminds me of thunder, and I always cover my ears. One special thing I wanted to see was the big bridge that went over the huge river. The water is always blue and looks so beautiful with all the boats with their different colors. Today, even though the water was gray, the boats were still beautiful when we went over the bridge.

Finally we reached the park, and I couldn't wait to get out and have a good stretch. The rain was falling lightly now, and I stuck my tongue out to see if I could taste the rain, but it had no taste. There was a fresh smell in the air, and I took long deep breaths. Then, suddenly, the sun came out! It was time for another fun part of the trip, eating and playing games.

I didn't see much of the journey going back because I was so tired, after a fun day at the picnic, that I fell asleep right away.

Meet the Author

Maurice B.
Grade: three
State: New York
Hobbies: swimming and biking
What he'd like to be when he grows up: a police officer

Yunmi and Halmoni's Trip

Read to find the meanings of these words.

e Glossary

bustling
customs
foreigner
passport
sightseeing
skyscrapers
vendor

VISITING ANOTHER COUNTRY

Traveling to another country can be a great adventure. In a big city, it's fun to wander through **bustling** streets full of people and to look up at tall **skyscrapers**. Many visitors go **sightseeing** to look at a country's famous places. Some visitors also learn how a country's **customs**, such as how people greet each other, may be different from their own. In the next story, a girl does many of these things when she travels to Korea with her grandmother.

▲ A **foreigner** must bring a **passport** when visiting other countries. A passport has a photo of a person and information about where that person is from.

▲ Seoul is a bustling city in South Korea.

◀ Many people visit the Kyungbok Royal Palace in Seoul.

▶ You can learn a lot about a place from the people who live and work there, such as a **vendor** selling items at a market.

187

As a child in Korea, Sook Nyul Choi loved to read about faraway places. When she was older, Choi moved to one of those places — the United States — to go to college. She now lives in Massachusetts with her two daughters. She loves both the United States and Korea, and her books often tell how these two countries are both the same and different.

Other books: *Halmoni and the Picnic, The Best Older Sister*

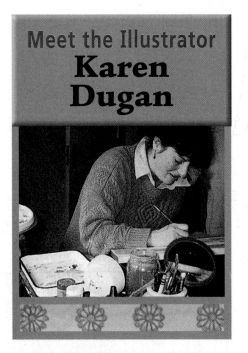
Karen Dugan has been making books since she was in first grade. She would fold paper into a book and then draw pictures. She doesn't fold her own pages anymore, but she still draws great pictures. For this book, she based the main character, Yunmi, on the author's daughters.

Other books: *School Spirit* (by Johanna Hurwitz), *Pascual's Magic Pictures* (by Amy Glaser Gage), *Halmoni and the Picnic* (by Sook Nyul Choi)

Internet

To find out more about Sook Nyul Choi and Karen Dugan, visit Education Place.
www.eduplace.com/kids

Yunmi and Halmoni's Trip

Sook Nyul Choi   *Illustrated by* Karen Dugan

Strategy Focus

Use your experiences of meeting new people to **predict** what might happen when a girl visits relatives she has never met before.

Yunmi settled into the airplane seat and took her grandmother's hand. It was Yunmi's first airplane trip. Her Halmoni, or grandmother, had come from Korea to take care of Yunmi while her parents were at work. Now Halmoni was taking Yunmi for a visit to Korea to meet all her aunts and uncles and cousins. Halmoni also wanted Yunmi to join Grandfather's birthday celebration. Yunmi's grandfather had died many years before, but each year the whole family visited his grave and celebrated his birthday.

Yunmi was very excited. She had gotten her very first passport for this trip. And she had promised to send lots of postcards to her best friends Helen and Anna Marie. It was a long flight from New York City across the Pacific Ocean to Seoul. It would take fourteen and a half hours. Halmoni, however, had lots of things to talk about during their flight. She pulled out a thick bundle of photos of Yunmi's many relatives, and began to tell her about each of them. Halmoni said, "I think they will all be at Kimpo Airport. They are so excited to meet you and want to show you all around Seoul."

When the airplane landed, they hurried through the airport to have their passports checked.

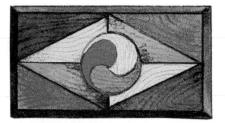

Halmoni walked Yunmi over to the long line that said "Foreigners." The line moved slowly as the officer checked each passport. Halmoni got to stand in the fast-moving line that said "Nationals." Yunmi looked like all the Koreans in the nationals line, but she had to stand in the foreigners line. It made her feel strange.

But when it was Yunmi's turn, the man checking passports smiled and said, "Welcome to Seoul. Are you here for a visit with your Halmoni?"

"Yes, how did you know?" asked Yunmi.

"I saw you talking with your Halmoni. She was my favorite high school teacher. I heard she went to America to be with her granddaughter. Please tell her Hojun said 'Welcome back.'"

Yunmi nodded happily. She wasn't a foreigner after all. People here already knew who she was. She was proud of Halmoni, too.

Halmoni was waiting for Yunmi, and they walked toward big sliding doors. Suddenly a huge crowd of people rushed toward them, waving and bowing. Yunmi stood still, her eyes wide. Everyone hugged her. Person after person bowed and embraced Halmoni. Halmoni was so happy, she had to wipe tears from her smiling face. Finally they walked past a long line of green and yellow taxis. An uncle ushered Halmoni and Yunmi into his car, and the rest of the relatives piled into cars and cabs.

They sped down broad highways, then through streets crowded with skyscrapers. In the middle of the city at the top of a narrow, winding street was a tall brick wall with a pretty iron gate. Inside was Halmoni's house. Halmoni's older sister, who lived there now, rushed out. A cat and a dog with a fluffy tail ran behind her. Halmoni embraced her sister and bent to pet her dog. "Oh, I missed you, too," she said to him. Then she lifted the cat onto her shoulder and carried her inside.

During the next several days, Yunmi's cousins Jinhi and Sunhi took her sightseeing. They went to the royal palace, called Kyong Bok Kung. Yunmi liked running down the center of the wide steps, where only the kings and queens and ministers had once been allowed to walk.

They visited the National Museum. There, Yunmi learned that in the seventh century, Koreans built the Chomsongdae Observatory to study the stars. She also learned that in the thirteenth century, Koreans were the first in the world to invent movable metal type to print books.

They went to the bustling East Gate Market. A street vendor there was baking little cakes filled with sweet red beans. Jinhi, Sunhi, and Yunmi each bought one and ate the cakes as they roamed the crowded stalls. "Socks for sale," "Silk shirts here," "Parasols on special," the vendors chanted as the girls walked past. Then Yunmi's cousins took her to their favorite stall.

There, Yunmi bought two soft lavender and pink silk purses with shiny black tassels for her friends Anna Marie and Helen. Yunmi was having fun with her cousins, but it was a little hard to understand their English. And when Yunmi spoke Korean, her cousins giggled and said she sounded funny.

Yunmi had hardly seen Halmoni since they arrived. Her grandmother was often out, and when she was home, Yunmi's cousins always sat on her lap and got all her attention. "Halmoni, don't ever leave us again," they kept saying. Halmoni just smiled. Yunmi sometimes wished everyone would disappear so she and Halmoni could talk like they did in New York.

For the next few days, Halmoni did stay home. But all Yunmi's aunts and cousins came over to prepare for the big picnic at Grandfather's tomb. They spent two whole days in the kitchen, making marinated beef, vegetables, dumplings, and sweets. Halmoni rushed about, overseeing everything.

"Sunhi," Halmoni said as she gave her a hug, "why don't you be in charge of making the mandoo? You can teach Yunmi. The dumplings are her favorite."

Halmoni rushed back with stacks of thin white dumpling skins, a bowl of water, and a big bowl of meat-and-vegetable filling. Sunhi placed just the right amount of filling on half of a dumpling skin. Then she dipped her pinky in the water and ran it around half the edge of the mandoo skin. She folded it into a half-moon shape and pressed the edge shut. Yunmi tried making them too. Soon they started making funny-shaped mandoo. Some looked like round balls, others like little purses, and some just looked strange. Halmoni smiled as she hurried past.

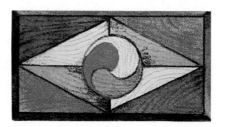

Yunmi saw how happy Halmoni was with all her family, and Yunmi started to worry. What if Halmoni didn't want to leave? In New York, Halmoni had only Yunmi and her parents and Yunmi's friends. She was scared, but tried to think about how much Halmoni loved her.

The next day was Grandfather's birthday. They loaded all the food and drink into big vans they had rented. Everyone, all the cousins and uncles and aunts, climbed in, and they sped toward the outskirts of Seoul where Grandfather was buried. As they rode through the big city streets and then the winding country roads, Yunmi and her cousins sang Korean songs, played cat's cradle, and folded paper into the shapes of birds and baskets.

They stopped at the bottom of a small mountain. Everyone got out and climbed all the way to the top, to a small field. In the middle was a little hill covered with soft green grass.

There on the hill was a large, flat stone with Grandfather's name on it. Below that were a lot of other names. Yunmi was surprised to see her parents' names and her name. Then she remembered Halmoni telling her it was a Korean custom to list the names of all the children and grandchildren on a tombstone. Yunmi went up and touched the cool stone and felt the warm sunlight on her hand. Meanwhile, Halmoni gathered the whole family. Together they made three deep bows to Grandfather.

Then Halmoni said, "Grandfather will be happy to see us all having a good time visiting him and each other on his birthday. Let's eat and celebrate this beautiful day." They sat down to a picnic with all the food they had prepared.

Yunmi had only been to a cemetery once before. She had seen people place flowers at a grave, say a prayer, and leave quietly. But in Korea, no one cried or looked sad. The cousins ran through the field collecting flowers and smooth stones for Grandfather's hill.

Yunmi wanted to talk with Halmoni, but everyone was crowded around her. Yunmi went and sat under a big tree all by herself to think. As she watched Halmoni, Yunmi grew more and more afraid that Halmoni would not want to go back to New York.

"Yunmi, help us look for more stones," said Sunhi.

"Why are you all by yourself?" Jinhi asked. "What's wrong?"

"Nothing. Nothing's wrong. Why don't you go sit with Halmoni. She's missed you all year," Yunmi said and burst into tears. She jumped up and ran, tears streaming down her cheeks.

When she couldn't run anymore, Yunmi threw herself on the grass and cried and cried. She imagined going back to New York all by herself, and all the lonely afternoons she would spend without Halmoni. She knew Halmoni was happy here, but it all seemed so unfair.

Soon she heard Halmoni's voice. "Yunmi, what's the matter?" She didn't answer.

Halmoni patted her. "Aren't you enjoying your visit? Everyone is so happy you're here. They wish you could stay longer."

Yunmi blurted, "They just want me to stay so they can keep you here. I know you want to stay. You're so happy and busy."

Halmoni sighed. "Oh, dear! Have I been that bad? I'm sorry. It's just that I want to take care of everything so I'll be ready to spend another year with you."

Yunmi looked up. "Another year with me?"

"Yes, Yunmi. Another year in New York, just as we planned."

Suddenly Yunmi felt ashamed and selfish. She stared down at the grass. "Halmoni, you have your house, your pets, and all your grandchildren and friends here. In New York, you only have my parents and me. If you want to stay, I understand."

Halmoni smiled. "I do miss everyone here, but I have a family I belong to in New York. And you have a family here too. We're lucky because we both have two families."

Yunmi thought of her cousins Sunhi and Jinhi. "Halmoni, I kept wishing all my cousins would disappear. They were so nice to me, and even helped me buy presents for my friends."

Halmoni stroked Yunmi's hair and said, "They like you so much, you are already one of their favorite cousins."

"Halmoni, do you think we can invite Jinhi and Sunhi to New York for a visit? I'd like to show them around," said Yunmi.

Halmoni smiled. "Oh, I know they would love to. Why don't you ask them?"

Yunmi heard her cousins calling. She took Halmoni's hand and helped her up. Together they walked over to join Yunmi's family.

Think About the Selection

 1. How does Yunmi feel about her relatives in Korea by the end of the story? Explain your answer.

2. Why do you think that celebrating Grandfather's birthday is so important to Yunmi and Halmoni's family?

3. In what ways does Yunmi change because of her visit to Korea?

4. How do you think Yunmi's cousins would feel about visiting Yunmi in the United States?

5. If someone came to visit you from far away, how would you make them feel welcome?

6. **Connecting/Comparing** Both Yunmi and the boy in *Across the Wide Dark Sea* take long voyages. Compare their experiences.

Narrating

Write a Personal Narrative

Have you ever taken a trip to visit relatives or friends? Write about a trip that you have taken. What made the visit exciting or difficult? Tell what was most interesting about your trip.

Tips

- To get started, make a story map of your trip.
- Be sure to keep the events in order.
- Use words that describe sights, sounds, and feelings.

Social Studies

Find Out Names for Grandparents

In a small group, list all the names you know for *grandmother* and *grandfather*. Include names from other languages if possible. Compare your group's results with the rest of the class.

Grandmother
Halmoni
Nonna

Grandfather
Abuelo

Listening and Speaking

Be a Tour Guide

Yunmi's cousins give her a tour of their town. Plan a tour of your classroom or school. In a small group, decide what places to show and what to tell about each one. Then ask permission to invite visitors to take the tour.

Tips

- Give everyone a chance to talk.
- Explain why different parts of your classroom or school are important.

Internet

Solve a Web Crossword Puzzle

What new words did you learn from *Yunmi and Halmoni's Trip*? Go to Education Place and print out a crossword puzzle about the selection. **www.eduplace.com/kids**

Journeys Through Art

Skill: How to Look at Fine Art

❶ **Look** at the whole painting or sculpture. **Think** about how it makes you feel.

❷ Then look more carefully. **Focus** on small details or parts. **Notice** colors and shapes.

❸ **Respond** to the art. Tell a friend how the art makes you feel or what it makes you think about.

Geese in Flight, **1850 or later**
Leila T. Bauman

The Seven **Ri** *Ferry Boat*
Approaching Kuwana, **1855**
Ando Hiroshige

Airplane Over Train, 1913
Natalia Goncharova

View of the Pont de Sèvres and the Slopes of Clamart,
St. Cloud, and Bellevue, **1908**
Henri Rousseau

Car, **1943**
Alexander Calder

213

Trapped by the Ice!

**Read to find
the meanings
of these words.**

e ● Glossary

barren

crevasse

floes

grueling

impassable

perilous

terrain

Exploring Antarctica

The continent located at the South Pole is called Antarctica. It is so cold in Antarctica that the land is **barren** — only a few plants and animals can survive there. The rough **terrain** is difficult to travel across.

Sir Ernest Shackleton explored Antarctica in the early 1900s. Traveling to Antarctica today would be **grueling**, but it was even more challenging for Shackleton's crew. They could never be sure whether they were walking on safe, solid ice or dangerous, moving ice **floes**. They never knew whether they might fall into a deep **crevasse** hidden under the snow and ice. And many times their path was completely blocked by **impassable** mountains or wild, icy seas. *Trapped by the Ice!* tells the story of this **perilous** voyage.

Sir Ernest Shackleton

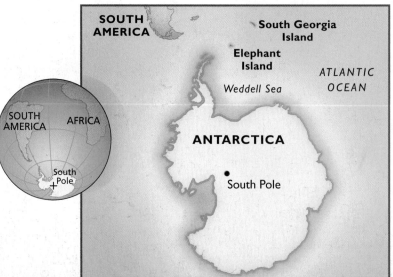

Michael McCurdy

Fact File

- Michael McCurdy has illustrated nearly 200 books, including classic stories such as *The Wonderful Wizard of Oz*. He has also written many books himself.

- In art school, McCurdy was a roommate of David McPhail, another children's author and illustrator.

- To create an illustration, McCurdy usually carves a picture on a wood block, covers the carving with ink, and stamps it on paper. But it's never too late to try something new — this story is the first book McCurdy has ever illustrated with paintings.

- McCurdy lives with his family in Massachusetts, where he works on his books in a big red barn. He enjoys playing the piano and hiking.

Internet

If you'd like to learn more about Michael McCurdy, stop by Education Place.

www.eduplace.com/kids

SHACKLETON'S AMAZING ANTARCTIC ADVENTURE

Trapped by the Ice!

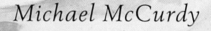

Michael McCurdy

Strategy Focus

Can Shackleton and his crew escape from the ice? **Monitor** your reading to make sure you understand what happens. Reread to **clarify**.

October 27, 1915

The *Endurance* was trapped. Giant blocks of
ice were slowly crushing her sides. From the deck,
Sir Ernest Shackleton looked at the snow and ice
that spread to the horizon. Ten months before, all
he had wanted was to be the first person to cross
the South Pole's ice cap.

Now his only concern was for his men. What
would happen to them — and how much longer
did the ship have before it broke apart? The
Endurance was leaking badly. Shack could not
delay.

Shack ordered his crew off the *Endurance* and
camp was set up on the frozen Weddell Sea. Tools,
tents, scrap lumber for firewood, sleeping bags, and
what little food rations and clothing the men had
left were saved from their ship, along with three
lifeboats in case they ever reached open water.

The *Endurance* was a sad sight now, a useless
hulk lying on its side. For months she had been
the crew's home. Now they would have to get used
to life on the ice — stranded hundreds of miles
from the nearest land.

November 21, 1915

Almost one month later, the sound of crushing wood startled the men. It was what they had feared. Turning toward the ship's wreckage, they saw her stern rise slowly in the air, tremble, and slip quickly beneath the ice.

220

Minutes later, the hole had frozen up over the ship. She was gone forever, swallowed by the Weddell Sea. Shack talked with the ship's skipper, Frank Worsley, and his next-in-command, Frankie Wild. Among them, they would have to decide what to do next.

December 23, 1915

Executing their plan would be difficult. By pulling the lifeboats, loaded with supplies, they would try to cross the barren ice to open water. If they made it, they would use the three boats to reach the nearest land. Shack studied the unending snow and ice ahead of him. Was it possible?

Each boat was mounted on a sledge. Harnessed like horses, the men pulled, one boat at a time. Pulling 2,000-pound loads was hard work. Soon everybody was so tired and sore that no one could pull anymore. The crew would have to wait for the ice, moved by the sea's current, to carry them north to open water.

Over the next few months, food was always a concern, and it was Tom Orde-Lees's job to find it. Penguins and seals were growing scarce. To find meat to eat, hunters had to go farther away.

This was dangerous. Once, when Tom was skiing back to camp, a monstrous head burst from the ice. A giant sea leopard lunged at Tom, only to slip quickly back into the dark water, stalking Tom from below, as sea leopards do when they hunt penguins.

Tom tripped and fell. The huge animal lunged again, this time springing out of the water and right onto the ice. Back on his feet, Tom tried to get away. He cried for help, and Frankie Wild rushed over from camp carrying a rifle.

The sea leopard now charged Frankie, who dropped calmly to one knee, took careful aim, and fired three shots. The sea leopard fell dead. There was plenty to eat for days afterward!

April 8, 1916

 The men smelled terrible. During their five and a half months on the ice they hadn't had a bath. Clothes were greasy and worn thin, and they rubbed against the men's skin, causing painful sores. Hands were cracked from the cold and wind, and hunger sapped everyone's strength.

 By now, the ice floes were breaking up into smaller and smaller pieces all around the men as they drifted closer to the edge of the polar sea. Shack thought it was a good time to launch the lifeboats, rigged with small canvas sails. He knew his men could not all survive the grueling 800-mile open-boat journey to the whaling station on South Georgia Island. So he decided to try to reach Elephant Island first.

11 p.m. April 8, 1916

Steering around the blocks of ice was hard. The boats bumped into ice floes — or crashed into icebergs. As night fell, the boats were pulled up onto a big floe and the tents were raised. But sleeping was difficult with damp bags and blankets, and with noisy killer whales circling around.

One night, Shack suddenly felt something was wrong. He shook Frankie, and they crawled out of their tent for a look. A huge wave smacked headlong into the floe with a great thud, and the floe began to split into two pieces. The crack was headed straight toward Tent Number 4!

Then Shack heard a splash. Looking into the crevasse, he saw a wriggling shape below in the dark water. It was a sleeping bag — with Ernie Holness inside! Shack acted quickly. Reaching down, he pulled the soggy bag out of the water with one mighty jerk. And just in time, too — within seconds the two great blocks of ice crashed back together.

April 13, 1916

Finally, the men reached open water. The savage sea slammed furiously into the three little boats — called the *James Caird*, the *Dudley Docker*, and the *Stancomb Wills*. Tall waves lifted them up and down like a roller coaster. Blinding sea spray blew into the men's faces. Most of them became seasick.

Worst of all, they were very thirsty, because seawater had spoiled the fresh water. The men's tongues had swelled so much from dehydration they could hardly swallow. Shack had his men suck on frozen seal meat to quench their thirst. They *had* to make land. They had to get to Elephant Island!

April 15, 1916

After an exhausting week battling the sea, the men nearly lost all hope. Big Tom Crean tried to cheer the men with a song, but nothing worked. Finally, something appeared in the distance. Shack called across to Frank Worsley in the *Dudley Docker*, "There she is, Skipper!" It was land. It was Elephant Island at last. It looked terribly barren, with jagged 3,500-foot peaks rising right up out of the sea, yet it was the only choice the men had.

April 24, 1916

Elephant Island was nothing but rock, ice, snow — and wind. Tents were pitched but quickly blew away. Without resting, Shack planned his departure for South Georgia Island. There he would try to get help. Twenty-two men would stay behind while Shack and a crew braved the 800-mile journey in the worst winter seas on earth.

The five ablest men were picked: Frank Worsley; Big Tom Crean; the carpenter, Chippy McNeish; and two seamen, Tim McCarthy and John Vincent. With frozen fingers and a few tools, Chippy prepared the *Caird* for the rough journey ahead. Only nine days after the men had first sighted the deserted island, Shack and his crew of five were on open water once again.

233

For the men who stayed behind, permanent shelter was now needed or they would freeze to death. Frankie Wild had the men turn the two remaining boats upside down, side by side. Then the boats were covered with canvas and a cookstove was put inside.

The hut was dark and cramped, lit only by a burning wick. And something happened that the men had not expected: heat from their bodies and the stove melted the ice under them as well as piles of frozen bird droppings left for years by the frigate birds and penguins. The smell was terrible!

Day after day the men looked toward the sea, wondering if Shack would make it back to rescue them. How long would they be left here? Was Shack all right?

May 5, 1916

The *Caird* made her way through the storm-tossed seas, while Shack and his men drank rancid seal oil to prevent seasickness. The ocean swelled and hissed and broke over the small boat as the men worried about the terrible graybeards found in these waters. Graybeards are monstrous waves that come quietly and quickly, threatening everything in their path.

The men had to battle to keep the boat free of ice, because any added weight might sink the *Caird*. Suddenly, Shack screamed from the tiller. The men turned around to face the biggest wave they had ever seen. It was a graybeard!

The boat shuddered on impact as the mountain of water spun it around like a top. Water filled the *Caird* while the men bailed furiously. Jagged rocks in her hull, which Chippy had used to keep the boat from capsizing, saved the day.

May 10, 1916

Finally, after seventeen grueling days at sea, young McCarthy shouted, "Land ho!" South Georgia Island lay dimly ahead. The whaling station was on the other side of the island, but the men had to land *now* or die. Their fresh water was gone, and they were too weak to battle the sea to the other side of the island.

While the men planned their landing attempt, they were hit by the worst hurricane they had ever encountered. For nine terrible hours they fought to keep afloat. Miraculously, just as things looked hopeless, the sea calmed enough to allow the *Caird* to land safely on the rocky beach of King Haakon Bay.

The men landed near a small cave with a freshwater spring
nearby. The cave would become a temporary home for John
Vincent and Chippy McNeish. Both had suffered too much on the
voyage and could not survive the long hike across the island to the
whaling station. Tim McCarthy stayed behind to take care of the
two sick men. Fortunately, water for drinking, wood from old
shipwrecks for fire, and albatross eggs and seals to eat meant those
who stayed behind would be all right while waiting for their rescue.

But Shack, Big Tom, and Skipper Worsley would have to climb over a series of jagged ridges that cut the island in half like a saw blade. All they could carry was a little Primus stove, fuel for six meals, fifty feet of rope, and an ice ax. Their only food consisted of biscuits and light rations that hung in socks around their necks. On their eighth day ashore, May 18, it was time to set off on the most dangerous climb they had ever attempted.

Three times the men struggled up mountains, only to find that the terrain was impassable on the other side. The men stopped only to eat a soup called "hoosh," to nibble on stale biscuits, or to nap five minutes, with each man taking a turn awake so that there would be someone to wake the others.

On and on the exhausted men hiked. From one mountain summit they saw that night was coming fast. Being caught on a peak at night meant certain death. They had to make a dangerous gamble. Shack assembled a makeshift toboggan from the coiled-up rope and the men slid 1,500 feet down the mountain in one big slide. Despite the perilous landing, they couldn't help but laugh with relief after they had crashed, unhurt, into a large snowbank.

The men had survived the long slide, but danger still lay ahead. They had been hiking for more than thirty hours now without sleep. Finally, all three heard the sound of a far-off whistle. Was it the whaling station?

They climbed a ridge and looked down. Yes, there it was! Two whale-catchers were docked at the pier. From this distance, the men at the station were the size of insects.

Shack fought against being too reckless. The three still had to lower themselves down a thirty-foot waterfall by hanging on to their rope and swinging through the icy torrents. At last, the ragged explorers stumbled toward the station. They had done it!

4 p.m. May 20, 1916

Thoralf Sørlle, the manager of the whaling station, heard a knock outside his office and opened the door. He looked hard at the ragged clothes and blackened faces of the men who stood before him. "Do I know you?" he asked.

"I'm Shackleton," came the reply. Tears welled up in Sørlle's eyes as he recognized his old friend's voice.

The three explorers received a hero's welcome from the whaling crew. The whalers knew that no one had ever done what Shack had accomplished. The next day, Skipper Worsley took a boat and picked up McCarthy, Vincent, and McNeish while Shack began preparations for the Elephant Island rescue.

It would take more than three months — and four attempts — to break through the winter pack ice and save the stranded men. But Shack finally did it — and without any loss of life. The men were glad to have a ship's deck once again under their feet. Finally, they were going home!

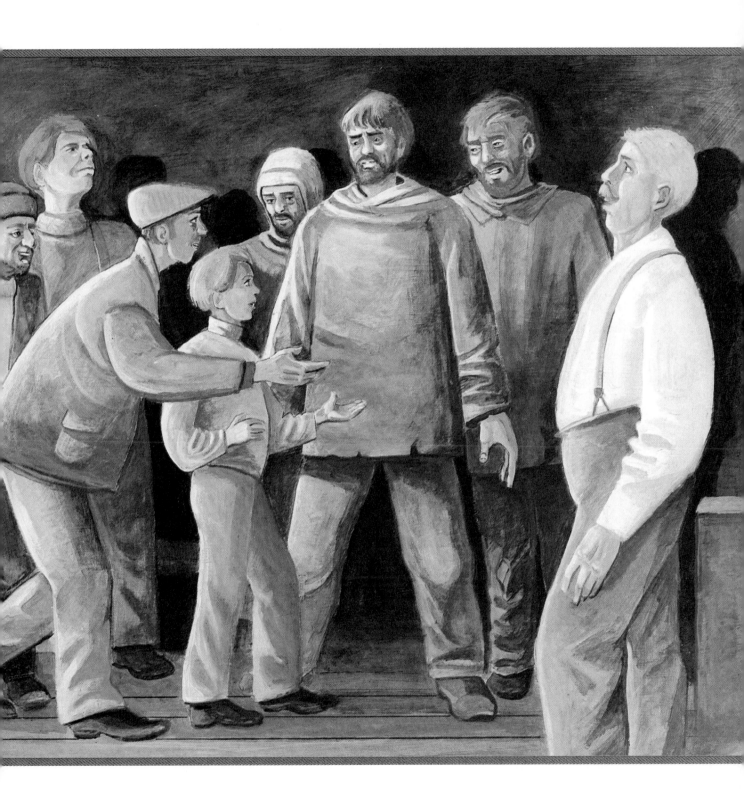

Think About the Selection

1. What do you think would have been the most difficult part of Shackleton's Antarctic voyage?

2. When Shackleton went to find help, how do you think the crew members who were left behind felt?

3. Name some qualities a person would need to survive a voyage like Shackleton's.

4. Would you have gone back with Shackleton to rescue the men on Elephant Island? Explain your answer.

5. Why do people call Shackleton a hero even though he didn't succeed in crossing the South Pole's ice cap?

6. **Connecting/Comparing** How is Shackleton's sea voyage like the *Mayflower* voyage? How is it different?

Informing

Write a Speech

Shackleton gave speeches telling people about his adventures. Choose a group Shackleton might have spoken to, such as reporters, other explorers, or students. Write a short speech Shackleton might have given to this group.

Tips

- Say *hello* and *good-bye* to the group. At the end, thank them for listening.
- Choose only a few parts of the voyage. Describe them in detail.
- Read your speech aloud to hear how it sounds.

246

Science

Investigate Ice

In a small group, talk about the way water freezes into ice and melts back into water. Then discuss the following questions.

- Why doesn't the stove melt the ice at the men's first camp? (pages 220–221)

- How can the ice carry Shackleton's crew north? (page 223)

- Why do the ice floes break up at the edge of the polar sea? (page 226)

Social Studies

Make a Timeline

Record Shackleton's journey on a timeline. On paper, draw a straight line. For each date, draw and label a dot on the line. Below each dot, write what happened on that date. Keep the events in order from left to right.

Bonus **Figure out when Shackleton began his journey and when he rescued the men on Elephant Island. Add these events to your timeline.**

Oct. 27, 1915

Take a Web Field Trip

You've read about three exciting voyages — now do some exploring of your own! Visit Education Place and link to Web sites for young travelers. **www.eduplace.com/kids**

Skill: How to Read a Photo Essay

❶ **Read** the title and introduction. **Scan** the photos.

❷ **View** the photos one at a time.

❸ **Read** the caption that describes each photo.

❹ **Note details** in the photos. Ask yourself what each photo shows you and how it helps you understand the topic.

Shackleton's Real-Life Voyage

Frank Hurley

The story of Shackleton's Antarctic journey is so amazing, it's hard to believe it really happened. But it did, and everyone survived. One crew member, Frank Hurley, even took photos during the voyage.

Hurley didn't know if he would return home. He wasn't sure if anyone would ever see his photos. However, he never gave up hope. He worked hard to protect the photos from ice, snow, water, wind, and freezing cold. Today, his photos still help people understand what this incredible adventure was like.

Hurley photographed the entire crew soon after the ship was caught in the ice.

The *Endurance* was slowly crushed by the powerful ice.

The crew tried to chop a path out of the ice. But the ice was too solid and thick, and there was too much of it.

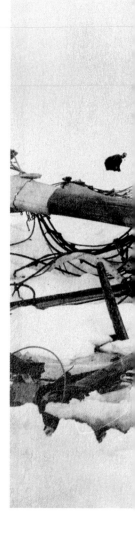

As the ice destroyed their ship, the crew had to camp in the freezing cold.

The crew pulled lifeboats and supplies across the icy terrain. It was grueling work.

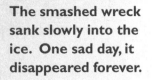

The smashed wreck
sank slowly into the
ice. One sad day, it
disappeared forever.

Rescued! Shackleton used a
rowboat to carry the twenty-two
men from Elephant Island to the
Yelcho, the ship in the background.
Finally, after nearly two years on
the ice, the crew traveled home.

Check Your Progress

In this theme, you have taken voyages all over the world. The next two selections that you'll read and compare will take you to two new places. You will also practice your test-taking skills.

Before you set sail, take a look back at Sook Nyul Choi's letter on pages 150–152. Which characters in this theme best show the courage that she talks about?

Now you're ready to read about a voyage by boat across the Pacific Ocean and a voyage by horseback and car across America. As you read, think about the courage the voyagers show.

Read and Compare

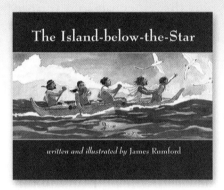

The Island-below-the-Star

written and illustrated by James Rumford

Find out how five brothers discover Hawaii.

Try these strategies:
Monitor and Clarify
Predict and Infer

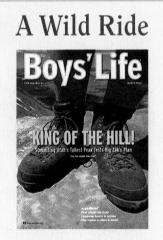

A Wild Ride

by Thomas Fleming

Ride along as two young brothers face a challenging journey across America to meet their hero.

Try these strategies:
Evaluate
Question

Strategies in Action *Try using all your reading strategies while you read.*

The Island-below-the-Star
written and illustrated by James Rumford

In the days when the stars were a map of the earth below, there lived on a tiny island in the South Pacific five brothers who loved adventure.

The first brother was Hōkū, and he loved the sun, the moon, and especially the stars.

The second was Nā'ale, and he loved the sea.

The third was 'Ōpua, and he loved clouds.

The fourth was Makani, and he loved the wind.

And the fifth was tiny Manu, and he loved birds.

One night, Hōkū said, "See, my brothers, that bright star there? There's an island below that star. Let us sail to it."

And as he spoke, the star sparkled with adventure.

Hōkū's four brothers looked up at the star over their own island and saw how very far away the other star was. No one had ever gone so far before.

Little Manu was first to speak. "I will go with you, Hōkū."

The other brothers, including Hōkū, laughed. Such a dangerous trip was out of the question for such a little boy.

"You might get washed overboard," said Nāʻale.

"Or frightened by the thunder and lightning," said ʻŌpua.

"Or blown away by the wind," said Makani. "Besides, you only care about birds."

The next morning, Manu stood watching as his four brothers prepared for their great trip without him to the Island-below-the-Star.

Hōkū dried bananas, taro, and breadfruit in the hot sun, for they would need much food.

Nāʻale fashioned dozens of fishhooks and readied the harpoons, for they would live off the sea as well.

ʻŌpua watched the clouds and gathered only the sweetest rainwater, for they would be thirsty on their long trip.

Makani repaired the sails, for they would need to catch even the tiniest breeze if they were ever to reach the Island-below-the-Star.

After several weeks, the canoe was seaworthy and the food and water were loaded on board. There was a great celebration for the four brothers.

Little Manu did not join in. No one noticed as he hid himself among the calabashes of food and baskets of coconuts.

The brothers left just before dawn.

It was sunset before they discovered little Manu.

"Let's toss him overboard and let him swim back," said Nāʻale.

"Let's throw him into the air and let the wind carry him home," said Makani.

Big ʻŌpua picked Manu up and held him over the side of the canoe.

"Hōkū!" cried Manu with his arms outstretched. "Hōkū!"

"All right! All right!" shouted ʻŌpua. "We were just kidding."

Hōkū began to laugh. "But you had better behave yourself," he told Manu.

Manu stood there, his head down.

"Make yourself useful," said Nāʻale. "We need fish."

Each day, as Manu sat with his fishing line, he was in awe of his brothers.

Hōkū used the sun, the moon, and the twinkling stars like a map to guide them.

When the clouds covered the heavenly map, they turned to Nāʻale, who kept the canoe on course as he felt the rhythms of the ocean waves.

'Ōpua was always there watching the clouds.

And when he predicted storms, Makani was at hand, disentangling the knotted wind as they sailed north to the Island-below-the-Star.

Several weeks later, it was Makani who first noticed a strange rush of warm air. He scanned the horizon.

The waves began to grow in strength as they slapped against the hull. Nāʻale alerted the others.

A thin palm frond of a cloud appeared above the horizon. 'Ōpua prepared his brothers for the worst.

By evening, the sky that Hōkū depended on was roiling with clouds. The waves were mountains. The wind was a knife.

The brothers tied a safety rope to Manu.

For five days and nights they hung on for dear life as they rode out the storm.

At last, the wind died down. The sea was calm, but the sky was still hidden behind a gray blanket of clouds. The canoe had been blown far off course. The brothers were lost.

Manu undid the safety rope. He had not cried when the thunder crashed through the sky. He had not been washed overboard or carried off by the wind.

Suddenly Manu stood very still. He could feel something coming.

He looked up and saw, perhaps on its way to the Island-below-the-Star, a tiny speck of a bird.

Manu called to his brothers, "Look, brothers, a bird! A bird on its way to land!"

"Where?" they cried. It was so high that they could not see it.

"Tell me where it is, Manu," said Hōkū. "Tell me which way to go."

Manu pointed in the direction the bird was flying, and Hōkū turned the canoe.

The bird stayed with the brothers all through the day, and Manu, proud Manu, told Hōkū of the bird's every turn.

That night, when the skies finally cleared, they all saw that they were beneath their star.

But where was the island?

Nā'ale showed them the waves crashing into one another, as though pushed back by something big.

'Ōpua pointed to the moonlit clouds gathered in the north as though caught by a mountain.

Makani told them how the wind was swirling oddly, as though avoiding some huge shape.

No one slept.

Manu, now part of the team, spotted the first birds in the predawn light.

They were close — very close.

And then, at dawn, they saw the island. Its peaks towered above the waves and caught the first rays of the rising sun. The brothers shouted with joy and lifted Manu high on their shoulders.

At noon, they found a quiet bay for the canoe.

At sunset, they set foot on shore.

That night, they gave thanks for their safe journey as they stood directly below the bright star that had called to them.

In the days when the stars were islands floating in a dark, heavenly sea and people were explorers living on specks of land surrounded by the vast ocean, they sang of

Hōkū, the star,

Nā'ale, the ocean waves,

'Ōpua, the cloud bank,

Makani, the wind, and

Manu, the bird, who found the Island-below-the-Star.

A Wild Ride

by Thomas Fleming

Bud Abernathy was ten years old and Temple Abernathy six when the brothers from Cross Roads, Oklahoma, decided they wanted to take a trip to New York — by themselves, on horseback — to see ex-President Theodore Roosevelt. Armed with a checkbook and permission from Dad, the boys started their long journey when the school year ended on April 5, 1910.

One Horse Down

Bud and Temple had been on the trail through Oklahoma's Indian Territory about two days when they got lost. The boys used the sun as a guide. It worked. They reached Oklahoma City and met their father for a day of sightseeing.

Their trip's first real trouble came a few days later in the town of Hominy. Temple led his horse, Geronimo, from the stable. Geronimo was slow and stiff. They stayed until the next morning, but Geronimo had not improved.

Bud had to rope another horse and pay $85 to the owner. That fee included the care of Geronimo until the boys could return.

Slogging Through Snow

Hard rain and mud slowed them from Hominy, through Coffeyville, Kansas, to the edge of the Ozark Mountains at Joplin, Missouri.

The bad weather was just beginning. As they rode north of Springfield, Missouri, the wind

Temple and Bud Abernathy ▲

became colder, and rain turned to snow. The boys got off their horses and walked for miles to stay warm and get a break from the wind. At times, the snow was so thick they could see only a few feet in front of them.

They reached Union, Missouri, on a Saturday night and sat in a hotel room all day on Sunday.

On Monday morning, despite the storm, they decided to leave for St. Louis, Missouri. By that night, they reached St. Louis and stayed for a week.

Through Sickness and High Water

The boys quickly made it through Illinois and Indiana. In Dayton, Ohio, they met Wilbur Wright and took a tour of the Wright airplane factory. Shortly after that, Temple got sick. He fought through a fever and lung infection in Cambridge, Ohio, and had to rest. A few days later, Bud was nearly swept downstream on his horse just outside Wheeling, West Virginia.

The next stop was Washington, D.C., where the boys met President William Howard Taft before reaching New York City. In New York, people knew who they were because of newspaper articles, and they were paid to appear in newsreel films. And they got to greet Mr. Roosevelt.

▼ **Theodore Roosevelt**

On the Road Again

For the journey from New York to Oklahoma, Bud persuaded his father to let them use their newsreel money to buy a car. There were no laws against boys driving in 1910, and there were only a few cars on the road.

The boys paid $485 for a Brush Runabout with a top speed of 30 miles an hour. Their horse ride took two months, their return car trip three weeks. They traveled more than 5,000 miles.

◄ **Bud and Temple in their brand-new car**

Think and Compare

1. Compare Manu's experiences of his voyage in *Island-below-the-Star* with Bud and Temple's experiences of their voyage across America. Use details from the selections.

2. Compare the importance of teamwork among the travelers in *Island-below-the-Star* and in *Trapped by the Ice!*

3. Which of the voyages in this theme would you most like to go on? Give two or three reasons.

4. Think of the characters in this theme. How do you think their experiences might change their lives?

Strategies in Action When did you use reading strategies in this theme? Tell how two or more of them helped you better understand the selections.

Persuading

Write a Radio Ad

Think about a place that you would like to travel to. Write a radio advertisement inviting people to go there. Tell why people should go, and what they will experience.

Tips
- Think about what visitors might see, hear, taste, smell, and touch.
- Use strong words, such as *certainly, really, of course.*

Taking Tests

 ## Writing an Answer to a Question

Some tests ask you to write an answer to a question about something you have read. Here is a sample test question for *Island-below-the-Star.*

Write your answer to this question.

Do you think the brothers will take another voyage together? Explain your answer.

---

1 **Understand the question.**

Find the key words in the question. Use them to help you understand what you need to do.

2 **Get ready to write.**

Skim the selection, using the key words. List the details that will help you answer the question.

Here is a sample planning chart.

Details About Brothers
1. They work well together.
2. They land safely.
3. They take care of each other.

266

Write your answer.

Use details from your list. Write a clear and complete answer.

Now read one student's answer.

> I think the brothers will go on another voyage together. They get along well and watch out for each other. The brothers did sail into a big storm, and maybe they were lucky to land safely. But I think that the way they look out for each other means that they will take another voyage together.

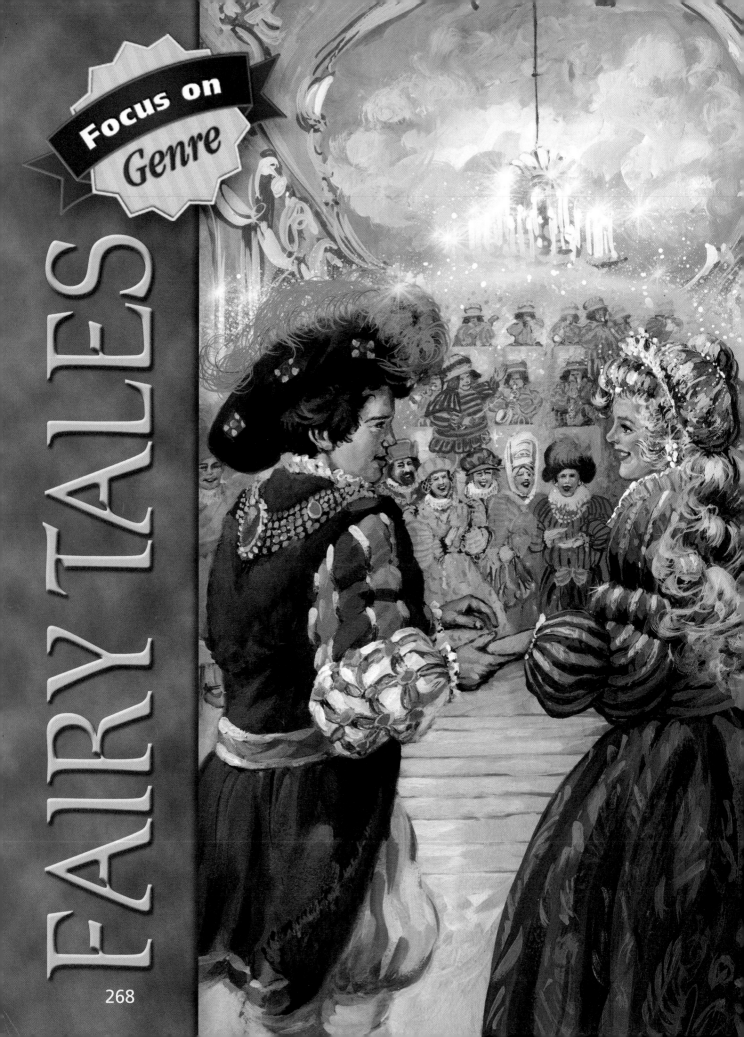

FAIRY TALES

Fairy Tales

A fairy tale is a kind of folktale that is hundreds of years old. Fairies sometimes do appear as characters. But you are more likely to find a **hero** or **heroine** with a problem to solve, events that cannot happen in real life, and a **happy ending**.

Here are two versions of the same fairy tale from two different cultures.

CONTENTS

269

Focus on Genre

Cinderella

by Charles Perrault, retold by Amy Ehrlich
illustrated by Robert Sauder

There once was a man whose wife died and so he took another. The new wife was proud and haughty, and had two daughters who were just like her in every way. But the man also had a daughter, and she was sweet and gentle and good as gold.

The wedding was hardly over before the woman began to make her stepdaughter's life a misery. From early morning until late at night the girl was forced to work, to scour the dishes and scrub the floors and pick up after her stepsisters. She did all she was asked and dared not complain to her father, who would only have scolded her, for his new wife ruled him entirely.

When she had finished her work, she used to go into the chimney corner and sit quietly among the cinders, and so she was called Cinder-wench. But the younger sister, who was not quite as rude as the others, called her Cinderella. In her ragged clothing with her dirty face Cinderella was yet a hundred times more beautiful than her stepsisters.

After some months had passed, the king's son gave a ball and invited to it all the stylish people in the countryside. The two sisters were also invited and immediately set about choosing the gowns and petticoats, the hair ornaments and slippers they would wear. This made Cinderella's work still harder, for it was she

who ironed their linen and pleated their ruffles. All day long the sisters talked of nothing but how they should be dressed.

One night, as Cinderella was helping them, they said to her, "Cinderella, would you not like to go to the ball?"

"Please, sisters, do not mock me," she said. "How could I ever dream of such a thing?"

"You are right," they answered. "People would surely laugh to see a Cinderwench at the ball."

For two days the sisters could hardly eat for excitement. So tightly did they lace themselves that they broke a dozen laces, and they were always at their looking glasses, trying on their gowns.

At last the evening of the ball came. Cinderella watched the sisters leave for the court, and when she had lost sight of them, she began to weep.

Her godmother, who was a fairy, saw her tears and asked what was the matter.

"I wish I could — I wish I could — go to the ball," stammered Cinderella, but she could say no more for crying.

"Well, then, go you shall," said her godmother. Then she told the girl to go into the garden for a pumpkin. Cinderella picked the finest she could find and carried it indoors. Her godmother scooped it out and struck it with her wand. Instantly the pumpkin turned into a fine gilded coach.

272

Next her godmother went to look in the mousetrap, where she found six mice, all alive. She tapped each one with her wand and they were turned into white horses, a fine set of them to draw the coach.

But they would still need a coachman, so Cinderella brought the rat trap to her godmother. Inside there were three rats. The godmother chose the one with the longest whiskers, and as soon as she touched him with her wand, he became a fat coachman with a most imposing beard.

After that the godmother turned six lizards into footmen, who jumped up behind the coach and held on as if they had done nothing else their whole lives.

Then her godmother said to Cinderella, "Well, my dear, here is your carriage. I hope it pleases you."

"Oh, yes!" the girl cried. "But am I to wear these rags to the ball?"

Her godmother simply touched Cinderella with her wand and at once her clothes were turned into a gown of silver. Then she gave Cinderella a pair of glass slippers, the most beautiful imaginable. But as the girl was making ready to leave, her godmother warned her that she must return home by midnight. If she stayed one moment longer, her coach would be a pumpkin again, her horses mice, her coachman a rat, her footmen lizards, and her clothing would turn back into rags.

Cinderella promised she would not be late and then she went off to the ball, her heart pounding for joy.

The king's son had been told that a great princess, unknown to all the company, would soon arrive, and he ran out to receive her himself. He gave her his hand as she sprang from the coach and led her into the hall where everyone was assembled. At once there was silence. So awed were the guests by the mysterious princess that they left off dancing and the musicians ceased to play. Then a hushed murmur swept the room:

"Ah, how lovely she is! How lovely!"

The king's son led her across the floor and they danced together again and again. A fine banquet was served, but the young prince only gazed at her and could not eat a bite.

After a time she left his side and went to sit by her sisters. She treated them with kindness and offered them sections of oranges that the prince had given to her. It very much pleased them to be singled out in this way.

Then Cinderella heard the clock strike a quarter to twelve. Quickly she wished the company good night and ran from the hall and down the palace steps to her coach.

When she was home again, she found her godmother and thanked her and asked if she might go to the ball again the next day. As Cinderella was telling her godmother all that had happened, her two sisters came into the room.

"If you had only been there," said her sisters. "There was an unknown princess, the most beautiful ever seen in this world. She sat with us and gave us oranges."

"Was she really so very beautiful? And do you not know her name?" Then Cinderella turned to the elder one. "Ah, dear sister, won't you give me your plainest dress so that I might see the princess for myself?"

"What? Lend my clothing to a dirty Cinderwench? I should be out of my mind!" cried the sister.

Cinderella had expected such an answer and she was very glad of the refusal. The next evening the two sisters went to the ball and she went too, dressed even more exquisitely than the first time. The king's son was always with her and spoke to her with words of praise. So entranced was Cinderella that she forgot her godmother's warning and heard the chimes of midnight striking when she thought it could be no more than eleven o'clock.

At once she arose and fled, nimble as a deer. Though the prince rushed after her, he could not catch her. In her haste she left behind one of the glass slippers, which he picked up and carried with him.

Cinderella's coach had vanished and she had to run home in the dark. Of her finery nothing remained but the other glass slipper. The guards at the palace gates were asked if they had seen a princess, but they replied that no one had come there but a poor country girl dressed in rags.

When the two sisters returned from the ball, Cinderella asked whether the unknown princess had again appeared. They told her yes but said she had hurried away the moment the clock struck midnight. And now the king's son had only the glass slipper she had left behind. They said he was brokenhearted and would do anything to find her once more.

All this was true. A few days afterward the king's son proclaimed that he would marry the woman for whom the glass slipper had been made. The couriers began by trying the slipper on all the princesses. They tried it on the duchesses and then on the ladies of the court. But nowhere in the land could they find a woman whose foot was small enough to fit the slipper. At last it was brought to the two sisters.

They pushed and pushed, trying to squeeze their feet inside, but they were not able to manage it.

Cinderella was in the room and recognized her slipper at once. "Let me see if it will fit my foot," she said.

Her sisters began to laugh and tease her. But the courier who'd been sent with the slipper looked at Cinderella and saw that she was lovely. He said his orders were that every woman in the land must try it on.

Cinderella sat down and he held the slipper up to her little foot. It went on at once, as easily as if it had been made of wax.

Then, while the two sisters watched, Cinderella drew from her pocket the other glass slipper and put it on too. Suddenly her godmother was there and she touched the girl's ragged clothes with her wand and they became a gown even more beautiful than the ones she had worn to the ball.

And now her two sisters knew she had been the unknown princess they had so admired. They threw themselves at her feet to beg her forgiveness for all their ill treatment. Cinderella bid them to rise and said that she forgave them with all her heart.

Then Cinderella was taken before the prince. He was overwhelmed with love for her and sometime later they were married. Cinderella, who was as good as she was beautiful, gave her two sisters a home in the palace, and that very same day they were married to two lords of the court.

Yeh-Shen

retold by Ai-Ling Louie, illustrated by Ed Young

In the dim past, even before the Ch'in and the Han dynasties, there lived a cave chief of southern China by the name of Wu. As was the custom in those days, Chief Wu had taken two wives. Each wife in her turn had presented Wu with a baby daughter. But one of the wives sickened and died, and not too many days after that Chief Wu took to his bed and died too.

Yeh-Shen, the little orphan, grew to girlhood in her stepmother's home. She was a bright child and lovely too, with skin as smooth as ivory and dark pools for eyes. Her stepmother was jealous of all this beauty and goodness, for her own daughter was not pretty at all. So in her displeasure, she gave poor Yeh-Shen the heaviest and most unpleasant chores.

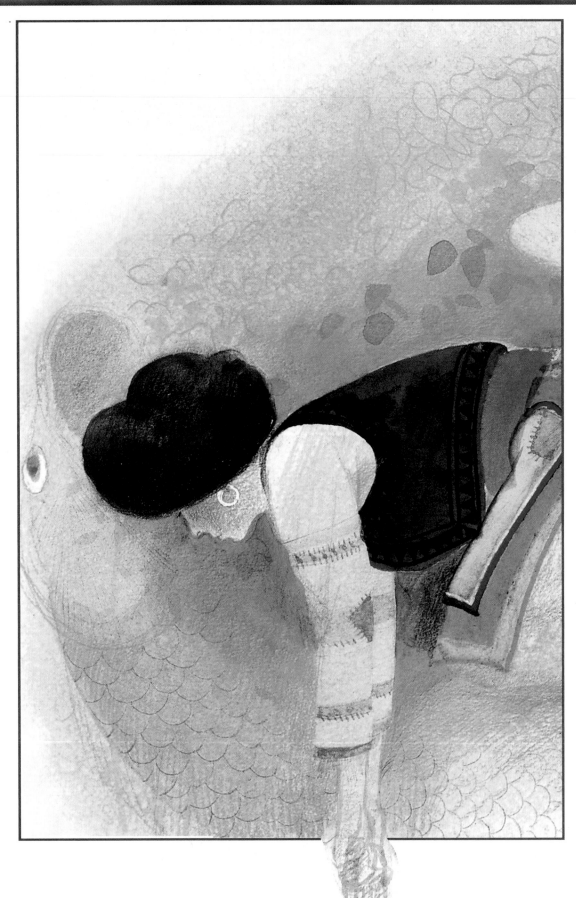

The only friend that Yeh-Shen had to her name was a fish she had caught and raised. It was a beautiful fish with golden eyes, and every day it would come out of the water and rest its head on the bank of the pond, waiting for Yeh-Shen to feed it. Stepmother gave Yeh-Shen little enough food for herself, but the orphan child always found something to share with her fish, which grew to enormous size.

Somehow the stepmother heard of this. She was terribly angry to discover that Yeh-Shen had kept a secret from her. She hurried down to the pond, but she was unable to see the fish, for Yeh-Shen's pet wisely hid itself. The stepmother, however, was a crafty woman, and she soon thought of a plan. She walked home and called out, "Yeh-Shen, go and collect some firewood. But wait! The neighbors might see you. Leave your filthy coat here!" The minute the girl was out of sight, her stepmother slipped on the coat herself and went down again to the pond. This time the big fish saw Yeh-Shen's familiar jacket and heaved itself onto the bank, expecting to be fed. But the stepmother, having hidden a dagger in her sleeve, stabbed the fish, wrapped it in her garments, and took it home to cook for dinner.

When Yeh-Shen came to the pond that evening, she found her pet had disappeared. Overcome with grief, the girl collapsed on the ground and dropped her tears into the still waters of the pond.

"Ah, poor child!" a voice said.

Yeh-Shen sat up to find a very old man looking down at her. He wore the coarsest of clothes, and his hair flowed down over his shoulders. "Kind uncle, who may you be?" Yeh-Shen asked.

"That is not important, my child. All you must know is that I have been sent to tell you of the wondrous powers of your fish."

"My fish, but sir . . ." The girl's eyes filled with tears, and she could not go on.

The old man sighed and said, "Yes, my child, your fish is no longer alive, and I must tell you that your stepmother is once more the cause of your sorrow." Yeh-Shen gasped in horror, but the old man went on. "Let us not dwell on things that are past," he said, "for I have come bringing you a gift. Now you must listen carefully to this: The bones of your fish are filled with a powerful spirit. Whenever you are in serious need, you must kneel before them and let them know your heart's desire. But do not waste their gifts."

Yeh-Shen wanted to ask the old sage many more questions, but he rose to the sky before she could utter another word. With heavy heart, Yeh-Shen made her way to the dung heap to gather the remains of her friend.

Time went by, and Yeh-Shen, who was often left alone, took comfort in speaking to the bones of her fish. When she was hungry, which happened quite often, Yeh-Shen asked the bones for food. In this way, Yeh-Shen managed to live from day to day, but she lived in dread that her stepmother would discover her secret and take even that away from her.

So the time passed and spring came. Festival time was approaching: It was the busiest time of the year. Such cooking and cleaning and sewing there was to be done! Yeh-Shen had hardly a moment's rest. At the spring festival young men and young women from the village hoped to meet and choose whom they would marry. How Yeh-Shen longed to go! But her stepmother had other plans. She hoped to find a husband for her own daughter and did not want any man to see the beauteous Yeh-Shen first. When finally the holiday arrived, the stepmother and her daughter dressed themselves in their finery and filled their baskets with sweetmeats. "You must remain at home now, and watch to see that no one steals fruit from our trees," her stepmother told Yeh-Shen, and then she departed for the banquet with her own daughter.

287

As soon as she was alone, Yeh-Shen went to speak to the bones of her fish. "Oh, dear friend," she said, kneeling before the precious bones, "I long to go to the festival, but I cannot show myself in these rags. Is there somewhere I could borrow clothes fit to wear to the feast?" At once she found herself dressed in a gown of azure blue, with a cloak of kingfisher feathers draped around her shoulders. Best of all, on her tiny feet were the most beautiful slippers she had ever seen. They were woven of golden threads, in a pattern like the scales of a fish, and the glistening soles were made of solid gold. There was magic in the shoes, for they should have been quite heavy, yet when Yeh-Shen walked, her feet felt as light as air.

"Be sure you do not lose your golden shoes," said the spirit of the bones. Yeh-Shen promised to be careful. Delighted with her transformation, she bid a fond farewell to the bones of her fish as she slipped off to join in the merrymaking.

That day Yeh-Shen turned many a head as she appeared at the feast. All around her people whispered, "Look at that beautiful girl! Who can she be?"

But above this, Stepsister was heard to say, "Mother, does she not resemble our Yeh-Shen?"

Upon hearing this, Yeh-Shen jumped up and ran off before her stepsister could look closely at her. She raced down the mountainside, and in doing so, she lost one of her golden slippers. No sooner had the shoe fallen from her foot than all her fine clothes turned back to rags. Only one thing remained — a tiny golden shoe. Yeh-Shen hurried to the bones of her fish and returned the slipper, promising to find its mate. But now the bones were silent.

Sadly Yeh-Shen realized that she had lost her only friend. She hid the little shoe in her bedstraw, and went outside to cry. Leaning against a fruit tree, she sobbed and sobbed until she fell asleep.

The stepmother left the gathering to check on Yeh-Shen, but when she returned home she found the girl sound asleep, with her arms wrapped around a fruit tree. So thinking no more of her, the stepmother rejoined the party. Meantime, a villager had found the shoe. Recognizing its worth, he sold it to a merchant, who presented it in turn to the king of the island kingdom of T'o Han.

The king was more than happy to accept the slipper as a gift. He was entranced by the tiny thing, which was shaped of the most precious of metals, yet which made no sound when touched to stone. The more he marveled at its beauty, the more determined he became to find the woman to whom the shoe belonged.

A search was begun among the ladies of his own kingdom, but all who tried on the sandal found it impossibly small. Undaunted, the king ordered the search widened to include the cave women from the countryside where the slipper had been found. Since he realized it would take many years for every woman to come to his island and test her foot in the slipper, the king thought of a way to get the right woman to come forward. He ordered the sandal placed in a pavilion by the side of the road near where it had been found, and his herald announced that the shoe was to be returned to its original owner. Then from a nearby hiding place, the king and his men settled down to watch and wait for a woman with tiny feet to come and claim her slipper.

All that day the pavilion was crowded with cave women who had come to test a foot in the shoe. Yeh-Shen's stepmother and stepsister were among them, but not Yeh-Shen — they had told her to stay home. By day's end, although many women had eagerly tried to put on the slipper, it still had not been worn. Wearily, the king continued his vigil into the night.

It wasn't until the blackest part of night, while the moon hid behind a cloud, that Yeh-Shen dared to show her face at the pavilion, and even then she tiptoed timidly across the wide floor. Sinking down to her knees, the girl in rags examined the tiny shoe.

Only when she was sure that this was the missing mate to her own golden slipper did she dare pick it up. At last she could return both little shoes to the fish bones. Surely then her beloved spirit would speak to her again.

Now the king's first thought, on seeing Yeh-Shen take the precious slipper, was to throw the girl into prison as a thief. But when she turned to leave, he caught a glimpse of her face. At once the king was struck by the sweet harmony of her features, which seemed so out of keeping with the rags she wore. It was then that he took a closer look and noticed that she walked upon the tiniest feet he had ever seen.

With a wave of his hand, the king signaled that this tattered creature was to be allowed to depart with the golden slipper. Quietly, the king's men slipped off and followed her home.

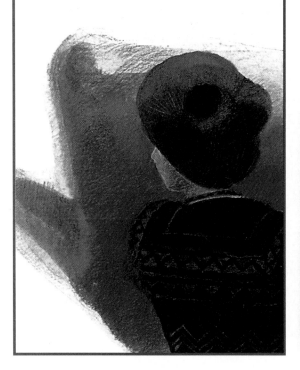

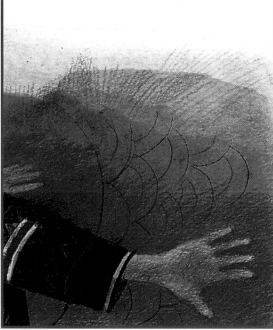

All this time, Yeh-Shen was unaware of the excitement she had caused. She had made her way home and was about to hide both sandals in her bedding when there was a pounding at the door. Yeh-Shen went to see who it was — and found a king at her doorstep. She was very frightened at first, but the king spoke to her in a kind voice and asked her to try the golden slippers on her feet. The maiden did as she was told, and as she stood in her golden shoes, her rags were transformed once more into the feathered cloak and beautiful azure gown.

Her loveliness made her seem a heavenly being, and the king suddenly knew in his heart that he had found his true love.

Not long after this, Yeh-Shen was married to the king. But fate was not so gentle with her stepmother and stepsister. Since they had been unkind to his beloved, the king would not permit Yeh-Shen to bring them to his palace. They remained in their cave home, where one day, it is said, they were crushed to death in a shower of flying stones.

Think About the

FAIRY TALES

1. Compare the two fairy tales. How are they alike? What are the most important differences between them?

2. If the fairy godmother and the fish bones didn't appear in the fairy tales, how else could the girls have solved their problems?

3. Who do you think is more of a heroine, Cinderella or Yeh-Shen? Why?

4. Compare how the tales end for the stepsisters. Do you think they get what they deserve? Explain.

Internet

Take an Online Poll

Do you like reading fairy tales? Which fairy tale is your favorite? Take an online poll at Education Place. **www.eduplace.com/kids**

Creating

Write a Fairy Tale

Think about how the two versions of Cinderella are alike and different. Write your own version of Cinderella. What will the characters be like? What problem will the main character have, and how will the problem be solved? Choose a setting. Your fairy tale can take place in a faraway castle, in a big city, or even in the ocean! You decide.

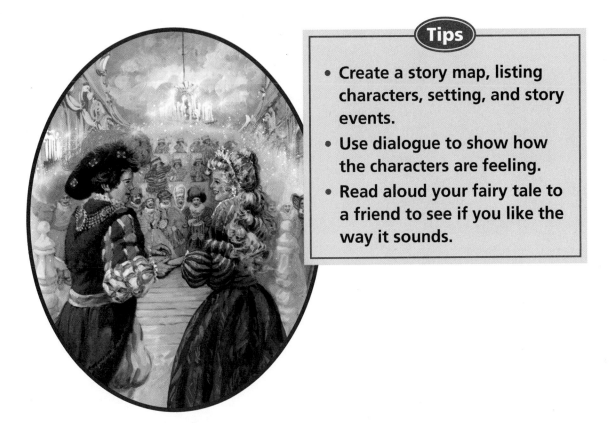

Tips

- Create a story map, listing characters, setting, and story events.
- Use dialogue to show how the characters are feeling.
- Read aloud your fairy tale to a friend to see if you like the way it sounds.

Theme

Smart
Solutions

If you run into a wall, don't
turn around and give up.
Figure out how to climb it, go
through it, or work around it.

Michael Jordan

Smart Solutions

with Ofelia Dumas Lachtman

People solve problems in different ways. Here is how Ofelia Dumas Lachtman solves a problem that you might have.

Dear Third-Graders,

What do you do when you're already on the school bus, and you find that you're wearing one bright blue sock and a striped, white one? What do you do when you're served a giant helping of green peas again, and you can't stand to eat even one?

Maybe the first thing you do is to wish that you were somewhere else. Or maybe your wish is for an instruction manual that tells you how to solve problems step-by-step.

Let's say that you have the "Oh, no, not green peas again!" problem. Wouldn't it be great to have a guide like the one on the next page?

How to Get Rid of Green Peas on Your Plate

Step 1 Count the peas. It's always good to know what you're up against.

Step 2 Spear two or three peas with a sharp-tined fork. Do not use a spoon. If you do, you will have run-about peas.

Step 3 Slip the peas off the fork into your pants pocket.

Step 4 Continue until all of the peas have disappeared from your plate. Do not press your pocket against your chair. Squish! Uh-oh! Forget it.

Step 5 Make a deal. Suggest that Mom or Dad choose three vegetables, and that you'll eat a full serving of one of them. Who knows? You may get one you actually like.

Step 6 As you munch on dessert, consider the possibility of using Step 5 as a way to solve other problems.

It's always good to find a solution to a problem, isn't it? And if it's a smart solution like the solutions in the stories you're about to read, that's even better.

Sincerely,

Ofelia Dumas Lachtman

How Smart Is That?

Think about Ofelia Dumas Lachtman's solution. How would you have solved the green pea problem?

Take a look at the book covers below. Think about what problems might be solved in these selections. As you read, decide if the solutions are good ones. Are there other ways to solve the problems?

Get ready to read about Poppa's pants, the Quimbys, and how a blind and deaf girl learned to communicate. They all have smart solutions.

Internet

To learn about the authors in this theme, visit Education Place. **www.eduplace.com/kids**

Pepita Talks Twice

Read to find the meanings of these words.

e Glossary

enchilada

languages

salsa

Spanish

taco

tamales

tortilla

Spanish Words

The girl in the story you are about to read speaks two **languages** — English and **Spanish**. You might be surprised to learn that many everyday words in English come from Spanish. Do you know the words *canyon*, *enchilada*, *plaza*, *rodeo*, *salsa*, or *tortilla*? If you do, then you know some Spanish. These are all Spanish words that have become part of the English language. Here are some other words that come from Spanish. Which ones do you know?

iguana

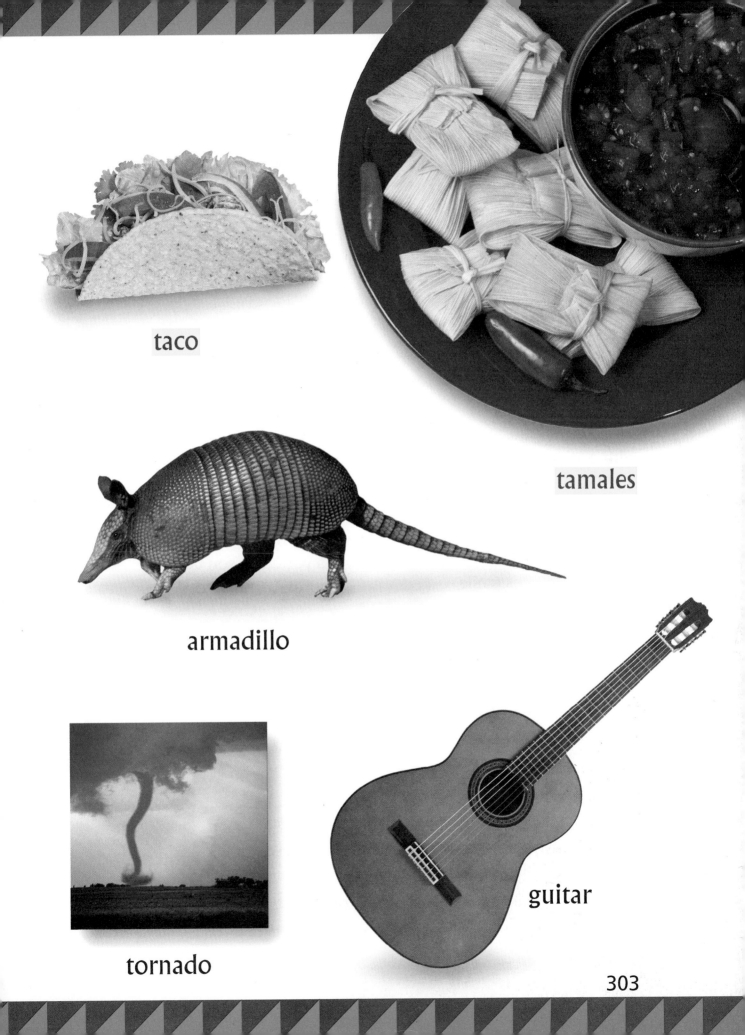

taco

tamales

armadillo

tornado

guitar

303

Meet the Author
Ofelia Dumas Lachtman

Meet the Illustrator
Mike Reed

Birthday: July 9

Where she lives:
Los Angeles, California

Favorite author as a child:
Louisa May Alcott, who wrote
Little Women

Where she gets her ideas:
"I get my best ideas from
scribbling, sometimes while
sitting under a tree."

Hobbies: walking, listening to
music, taking care of her cats

Other books: *Pepita Thinks
Pink/Pepita y el color rosado*

Birthday: August 22

Where he grew up:
Northville, Michigan

Where he lives now:
Minneapolis, Minnesota

His sons: Alex and Joseph

His dog: named Mousse
by his youngest son because
"he's brown and sweet"

Other books:

Christopher (by Lauren Wohl)

Space Dogs from the Planet K-9
    (by Joan Holub)

Taming the Wild Waiyuuzee
    (by Rita Williams-Garcia)

Internet

If you want to learn more about Ofelia Dumas
Lachtman and Mike Reed, visit Education Place.
www.eduplace.com/kids

Pepita Talks Twice
Pepita habla dos veces

By Ofelia Dumas Lachtman

Skipping Stones Honor Award

Strategy Focus

As you find out why Pepita has to talk twice, **evaluate** how the author makes Pepita and her problem seem real to you.

Pepita was a little girl who spoke Spanish and English.

"Come, Pepita, please help us," people would say. Everybody called on Pepita to talk for them in Spanish and English. And she did what they asked without a grumble. Until today.

Today she didn't want to help anyone. She wanted to get home before her brother Juan [HWAN]. She wanted to teach their dog Lobo a new trick. She wanted to teach him to fetch a ball. But if she didn't hurry, Juan would teach Lobo first.

Pepita era una niña pequeña que hablaba español e inglés.

—Ven acá, Pepita. Ayúdanos, por favor —le decía la gente. Todo el mundo llamaba a Pepita para que hablara por ellos en español y en inglés. Y ella hacía lo que le pedían sin quejarse. Hasta hoy.

Hoy, Pepita no tenía ganas de ayudar a nadie. Quería llegar a casa antes que su hermano Juan. Quería enseñarle un nuevo truco a su perro Lobo. Quería enseñarle a recoger la pelota. Y si Pepita no se apuraba, Juan se lo iba a enseñar a Lobo primero.

Pepita raced by the grocery store that belonged to Mr. Hobbs, but not fast enough. "Pepita," Mr. Hobbs called. "Come speak to this lady in Spanish. Tell me what she wants!"

Pepita did what Mr. Hobbs asked. But deep inside of her a grumble began.

She tiptoed by the house where her Aunt Rosa lived, but not softly enough. "Pepita," her aunt called in Spanish. "Come talk to the delivery man in English. Tell me what he wants!"

Pepita did what Aunt Rosa asked. But deep inside of her the grumble grew.

Pepita salió corriendo por la tienda de Mr. Hobbs, pero no pudo escaparse a tiempo. —Pepita —Mr. Hobbs la llamó—. Ven para que le hables a esta señora en español. ¡Dime lo que quiere!

Pepita hizo lo que Mr. Hobbs le pedía, pero muy por dentro sintió el principio de una queja.

Pasó en puntillas por la casa donde vivía su Tía Rosa, pero no pasó sin hacer un poco de ruido. —Pepita, ven a hablarle al repartidor en inglés. ¡Mira a ver qué quiere!

Pepita hizo lo que su tía le pidió, pero muy por dentro la queja se fue haciendo más fuerte.

She ducked behind the fence as she went by her neighbors' house, but not low enough.

"Pepita," Miguel called and said in Spanish, "my mother wants you to talk on the telephone in English. Please tell her what the man wants."

Pepita did what Miguel asked. But deep inside of her the grumble grew larger.

And when she went into her own yard and found her brother Juan teaching Lobo to return a ball, the grumble grew so big that it exploded.

"If I didn't speak Spanish and English," she burst out, "I would have been here first!"

Se deslizó detrás de la cerca de sus vecinos con la cabeza agachada, pero no la bajó lo suficiente.

—Pepita —Miguel la llamó y le dijo en español— mi madre quiere que hables por teléfono en inglés. Por favor, ven a ver lo que el hombre quiere.

Pepita hizo lo que Miguel le pidió, pero muy por dentro la queja se hizo más fuerte todavía.

Y cuando entró en su propio jardín y encontró que su hermano Juan ya estaba enseñándole a Lobo a recoger la pelota, la queja se volvió tan fuerte que explotó.

—¡Si yo no hablara español e inglés —exclamó—, habría llegado aquí primero!

That night as Pepita lay in bed, she thought and thought. By morning she had decided what she would do. She slipped out of bed and tiptoed by Lobo, who was sleeping on the floor. She hurried into the kitchen, where her mother was cooking breakfast and Juan was eating.

"I am never, ever going to speak Spanish anymore," Pepita said loudly.

"That's pretty dumb," Juan said.

"My, oh my, Pepita. Why?" her mother asked.

"Because I'm tired of talking twice."

"Twice?" her mother asked.

"Yes! Once in Spanish and once in English. So I'm never going to speak Spanish anymore."

Esa noche, ya en cama Pepita se puso a pensar y pensar. Cuando amaneció, ya había decidido lo que iba a hacer. Deslizándose de la cama, pasó en puntillas junto a Lobo, que dormitaba en el piso. Entró rápidamente en la cocina, donde su madre estaba preparando el desayuno y Juan estaba comiendo.

—Nunca más voy a volver a hablar español —Pepita dijo en voz muy alta.

—Ésa es una gran tontería —Juan le dijo.

—¡Ay, ay, Pepita! ¿Por qué? —le dijo su mamá.

—Porque estoy cansada de hablar dos veces.

—¿Cómo dos veces? —su madre le preguntó.

—¡Sí! Primero en inglés y después en español. Así que no voy a hablar más en español.

Juan took a bite of tortilla and grinned. "How will you ask for enchiladas and tamales . . . and tacos with salsa?" he asked. "They are all Spanish words, you know."

"I will find a way," Pepita said with a frown. She hadn't thought about that before.

After breakfast, Pepita kissed her mother, picked up her lunch box, and started to school. Outside, she put her lunch box down and closed the gate to the fence, but not tight enough. Lobo pushed the gate open and followed at her heels.

"Wolf," Pepita scolded, "go home!" But Lobo just wagged his tail and followed her to the corner.

Juan mordió un pedazo de tortilla y se sonrió. —¿Cómo vas a pedir enchiladas y tamales . . . y tacos con salsa? —preguntó—. Todas ésas son palabras españolas, ¿sabes?

—Buscaré la forma —Pepita dijo arrugando la frente. No había pensado en eso antes.

Después de desayunar, Pepita besó a su madre, recogió la lonchera con su almuerzo y salió para la escuela. Afuera, bajó la lonchera al suelo y cerró la verja del jardín, pero no del todo. Lobo abrió la verja de un empujón y la siguió.

—Wolf —Pepita lo regañó—, go home!— Pero Lobo le meneó la cola y la siguió hasta la esquina.

315

"Mr. Jones," Pepita said to the crossing guard, "will you please keep Wolf for me? If I take him back home, I'll be late for school."

"I'll walk him home when I'm through," Mr. Jones said. "But I thought his name was Lobo?"

"No," Pepita said. "His name is Wolf now. I don't speak Spanish anymore."

"That's too bad," said Mr. Jones, picking up his red stop sign. "I thought it was a good thing to speak two languages."

"It's not a good thing at all, Mr. Jones. Not when you have to speak twice!"

—Mr. Jones —Pepita le dijo al guardia de cruce—, ¿puede guardarme a Wolf? Si lo llevo a casa otra vez, voy a llegar tarde a la escuela.

—Yo te lo llevaré a casa cuando termine —Mr. Jones le dijo—. Pero yo creía que su nombre era Lobo.

—No —Pepita le dijo—. El se llama Wolf ahora. Yo ya no hablo español.

—¡Qué lástima! —dijo Mr. Jones tomando su letrero rojo de "Alto"—. Yo creía que era bueno hablar dos lenguas.

—No es nada bueno, Mr. Jones. No cuando uno tiene que hablar dos veces.

At school her teacher, Miss García, smiled and said, "We have a new student starting today. Her name is Carmen and she speaks no English. We must all be as helpful as we can."

Miss García looked at Pepita and said, "Pepita, please tell Carmen where to put her lunch and show her where everything is."

Carmen smiled at Pepita and Pepita just wanted to run away and hide. Instead, she stood up and said, "I'm sorry, Miss García, but I can't. I don't speak Spanish anymore."

"That is really too bad," her teacher said. "It's such a wonderful thing to speak two languages."

Pepita mumbled to herself, "It is not a wonderful thing at all, not when you have to speak twice!"

En la escuela, la maestra, Miss García, se sonrió y dijo:
—Tenemos una nueva alumna comenzando hoy. Se llama Carmen y no habla inglés. Todos debemos de ayudarla lo más que podamos.

Miss García miró hacia Pepita y le dijo: —Pepita, por favor, dile a Carmen donde puede poner su almuerzo y donde está todo.

Carmen le sonrió a Pepita y Pepita tuvo ganas de salir corriendo y esconderse, pero se levantó y dijo en inglés: —Lo siento, Miss García, pero no puedo. Yo ya no hablo español.

—¡Qué lástima! —dijo la maestra—. Es tan maravilloso hablar dos lenguas.

Pepita murmuró entre dientes: —¡No es nada maravilloso, no cuando uno tiene que hablar dos veces!

When Pepita walked into her yard after school, she found Lobo sleeping on the front porch. "Wolf, come here!" she called. "Wolf, wake up!" But he didn't open an eye or even wiggle an ear.

From the sidewalk behind her, Juan shouted, "¡Lobo! ¡Ven acá!" Like a streak, Lobo raced to the gate and barked.

Juan laughed and said, "Hey, Pepita, how are you going to teach old Lobo tricks if you don't speak Spanish?"

"I'll find a way," Pepita said with a frown. She had not thought about this either.

Cuando Pepita entró en su jardín al regresar de la escuela, encontró a Lobo durmiendo en el portal. —¡Wolf, ven acá, despiértate! —le dijo en inglés. Pero el perro no abrió ni un ojo ni meneó una oreja.

Desde la acera, Juan gritó en español: —¡Lobo! ¡Ven acá! —Lobo salió disparado hacia la verja, ladrando.

Juan se rió y dijo: —Oye, Pepita, ¿cómo vas a enseñarle trucos a Lobo si tú no hablas español?

—Ya buscaré la forma —Pepita dijo arrugando la frente. No había pensado en esto tampoco.

Pepita's neighbor Miguel was on the sidewalk bouncing a rubber ball. His brothers and sisters were sitting on their front porch singing. When they saw her, they called, "Come, Pepita! Sing with us!"

"I can't," she called. "All of your songs are in Spanish, and I don't speak Spanish anymore."

"Too bad," they said. "How will you help us sing at the birthday parties?"

"I'll find a way," Pepita said with a frown. This was something else she had not thought about.

El vecino de Pepita, Miguel, estaba en la acera jugando con una pelota de goma. Sus hermanos estaban sentados en el portal cantando. Cuando la vieron, la llamaron: —¡Ven, Pepita! ¡Ven a cantar con nosotros!

—No puedo —respondió—. Todas las canciones de ustedes son en español y yo ya no hablo español —dijo en inglés.

—¡Qué lástima! —dijeron—. ¿Cómo vas a poder cantar con nosotros en las fiestas de cumpleaños?

—Buscaré la forma —Pepita dijo arrugando la frente. Esto era algo más que no había pensado.

At the supper table, Pepita's mother told everyone that Abuelita [ah-bweh-LEE-ta], their grandmother, was coming the next day. "Abuelita says she has a new story for Pepita."

Juan laughed. "Abuelita tells all her stories in Spanish. What are you going to do now?"

"Nothing," said Pepita. "I can listen in Spanish."

"¿Qué pasa? ¿Qué pasa?" Pepita's father said. "What is going on?"

Pepita swallowed hard. "I don't speak Spanish anymore, Papá," she said.

"Too bad," her father said. "It's a fine thing to know two languages."

"It's not a fine thing at all," Pepita said and then stopped. Her father was frowning at her.

En la mesa a la hora de comer, la madre de Pepita le dijo a todos que Abuelita iba a llegar al día siguiente. —Abuelita me dice que tiene un cuento nuevo para Pepita.

Juan se rió. —Abuelita cuenta todos sus cuentos en español. ¿Cómo te las vas a arreglar ahora?

—No importa —dijo Pepita en inglés—. Puedo escuchar en español.

—¿Qué pasa? ¿Qué pasa? —el padre de Pepita dijo en español—. What's going on? —dijo luego en inglés.

Pepita tragó con dificultad. —I don't speak Spanish anymore, Papá —dijo.

—¡Qué lástima! —dijo su padre—. Es muy bueno saber dos lenguas.

—No es nada bueno —Pepita dijo y luego se detuvo. Su papá la miraba, arrugando la frente.

324

"She even calls Lobo 'Wolf'!" Juan said.

"Wolf?" her father said, and his frown grew deeper. "Well then, Pepita, we'll have to find a new name for you, won't we? How will you answer to Pepita if that is no longer your name?"

"I'll find a way," Pepita said with a long sad sigh. This was something she had never ever thought about before.

That night when she went to bed, Pepita pulled the blankets up to her chin and made a stubborn face. "I'll find a way," she thought. "If I have to, I can call myself Pete. I can listen in Spanish. I can hum with the singing. I can call a taco a crispy, crunchy, folded-over, round corn sandwich! And Wolf will have to learn his name!" With that she turned over and went to sleep.

—¡Hasta le dice 'Wolf' a Lobo! —Juan dijo.

—¿'Wolf'? —dijo su padre con aún más arrugas en la frente. —Bueno, Pepita, entonces vamos a tener que encontrarte un nombre nuevo. ¿Cómo vas a responder a 'Pepita' si ése ya no es tu nombre?

—Ya buscaré la forma —Pepita dijo suspirando muy hondo. Esto era algo que nunca había pensado antes.

Esa noche cuando se acostó, Pepita estiró las cobijas hasta la barbilla y puso una cara de terca. —Buscaré la forma —dijo—. Si quiero, puedo ponerme el nombre de Pete. Puedo escuchar en español. Puedo tararear cuando canten. Puedo llamarle al taco sandwich redondo de maíz doblado, tostado y crujiente. ¡Y Wolf tendrá que aprenderse su nombre!— Con esto se dio la vuelta y se durmió.

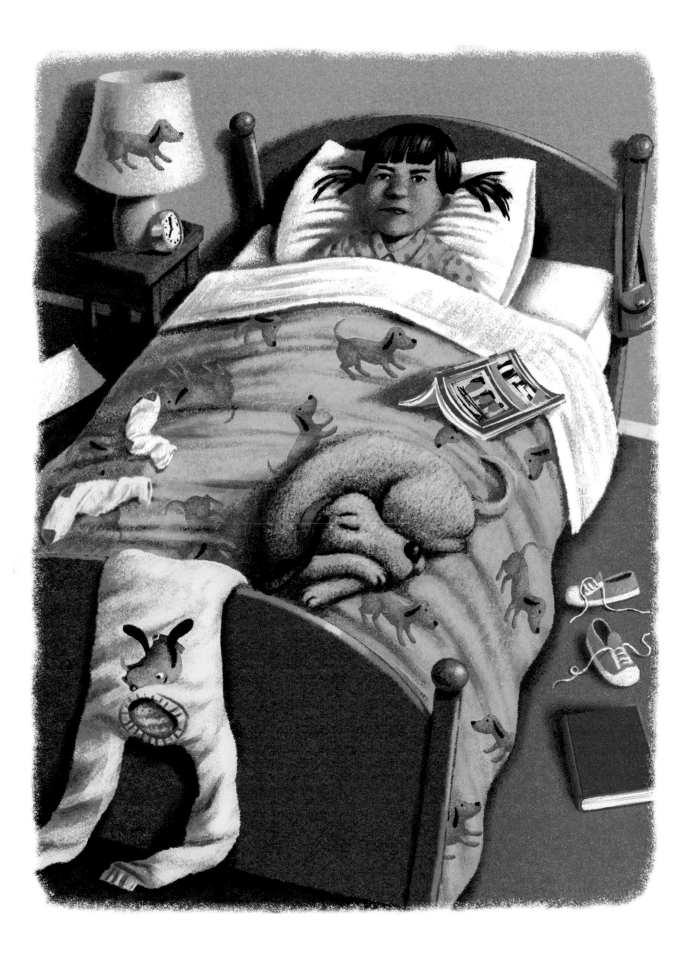

In the morning, when Pepita was leaving for school, her friend Miguel threw his ball into her yard. Lobo fetched it and dropped it at Pepita's feet.

"You're a good dog, Wolf," she said.

She put her lunch box down and threw the ball back to Miguel. The little boy laughed and clapped his hands. Just as she was opening the gate, he threw the ball again. This time it went into the street. Like a flash, Lobo ran after it.

"Wolf!" Pepita yelled. But Lobo didn't listen and went through the gate.

"Wolf! Come here!" Pepita shouted. But Lobo darted right into the street.

A car was coming!

Por la mañana, cuando Pepita iba a salir para la escuela, su amigo Miguel tiró su pelota al jardín de Pepita. Lobo la recogió y la dejó caer a los pies de Pepita.

—Eres un buen perro, Wolf —dijo ella en inglés.

Pepita colocó la lonchera en el suelo y le tiró la pelota de vuelta a Miguel. El niñito se rió y aplaudió. En el mismo momento en que Pepita abría la verja, Miguel volvió a tirarle la pelota. Esta vez cayó en la calle. Lobo corrió disparado a buscarla.

—Wolf! —Pepita gritó. Pero Lobo no le prestó atención y salió por la verja.

—Wolf! Come here! —Pepita gritó. Pero Lobo corrió hasta la misma calle.

¡Un automóvil se aproximaba!

Pepita closed her eyes. "¡Lobo!" she screamed. "¡Lobo! ¡Ven acá!"

Lobo turned back just before a loud screech of the car's brakes. Pepita opened her eyes in time to see the ball roll to the other side of the street. A red-faced man shouted out the window of the car, and Lobo raced back into the yard!

Pepita shut the gate firmly behind Lobo and hugged him. "Lobo, oh, Lobo, you came when I called in Spanish!"

She nuzzled her face in his warm fur. "I'll never call you Wolf again," she said. "Your name is Lobo. Just like mine is Pepita. And, oh, Lobo, I'm glad I talked twice! It's great to speak two languages!"

Pepita cerró los ojos. —¡Lobo! —gritó en español—. ¡Lobo! ¡Ven acá!

Lobo dio la vuelta un instante antes de que los frenos del automóvil chillaran. Cuando Pepita abrió los ojos, la pelota rodaba hacia el otro lado de la calle. Un hombre con la cara roja de furia gritaba por la ventanilla de su carro y Lobo regresaba corriendo al jardín.

Pepita cerró la verja firmemente detrás de Lobo y lo abrazó. —¡Lobo, oh, Lobo, viniste cuando te llamé en español!

Pepita escondió la cara en el pelaje caliente del perro. —Nunca más te llamaré Wolf —dijo—. Tu nombre es Lobo, como el mío es Pepita. Y ¡oh, Lobo, cómo me alegro de haber hablado dos veces! ¡Qué maravilloso es hablar dos lenguas!

Think About the Selection

1. What makes Pepita grumble at the beginning of the story?

2. In what ways do other people help Pepita change the way she thinks about her problem?

3. Why do you think the author made Lobo so important to the story?

4. After reading this story, what do you think is the best part of speaking two languages?

5. What new languages would you like to learn? Explain your answer.

6. **Connecting/Comparing** Which of Pepita's decisions do you think was a smart solution? Give reasons for your answer.

Persuading

Write an Opinion

What do you think of Pepita's actions? Did she do the right thing when she stopped speaking Spanish? What else could she have done to solve her problem? Write your opinion and then share it with a classmate.

Tips

- Focus on one or two of Pepita's decisions.
- State your opinion in a respectful way.
- Use phrases such as *I think* or *It seems to me*.

Perform a Reader's Theater

In a small group, choose two or three scenes from the story to read aloud. Plan who will play each part, including the narrator. Practice reading your parts with each other. Then present your scenes to the class.

Tips

- Speak slowly and clearly.
- Use expression in your face and voice.
- Let other readers finish their lines before you start yours.

Label Your Classroom

Make Spanish labels for things in your classroom. On a self-stick note, write a Spanish word from the list below. Put the note near the item that it names. Do the same for the other words on the list.

Bonus Use a Spanish/English dictionary to create more labels for your classroom.

el libro

Spanish	English
el pizarrón	chalkboard
el escritorio	desk
la silla	chair
la ventana	window
el papel	paper
el lápiz	pencil
el libro	book
el almuerzo	lunch

Internet

Solve a Spanish Mystery Grid

Learn some Spanish counting words. Visit Education Place and solve a puzzle in Spanish and English! **www.eduplace.com/kids**

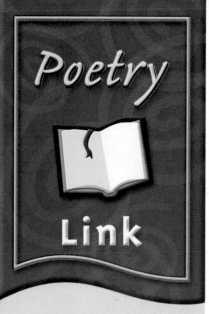
Skill: How to Read a Poem

❶ **Read** the poem several times. Look for patterns, such as rhythm or rhyme, in the words.

❷ Sometimes the same poem is written in two languages. **Look** at the poem in both languages. **Compare** titles, number of words, and punctuation.

❸ **Think** about what idea or feeling the poet is trying to express.

Little Piece of Prickly Pear

Mama calls me her little piece of prickly pear
when I am sour, when I stamp my feet.

Mama calls me her little *tuna*, good enough to eat
when I am smiling, when I am sweet.

Pedacito de nopal

Mamá me dice "pedacito de nopal"
cuando me enojo, cuando pataleo.

Mamá me dice "tunita" y me comería a besos
cuando sonrío, cuando soy tierna.

Tony Johnston

I Like to Ride My Bike

I'm ready
for a bike ride. I wear
long blue shorts, my red helmet and
a white T-shirt hanging to my knees.
One pedal
spins
and then, I'm off!

Leaves blur into green air
people shout hello, be careful
stay on the sidewalk.

The wind cools my arms
and legs.
I feel free.

Me gusta montar mi bicicleta

Estoy lista para mi paseo en bicicleta. Llevo
mis largas bermudas azules, mi casco rojo y
una camiseta blanca colgando hasta las rodillas.
Un pedal
gira
y luego, ¡parto!

Las hojas se desvanecen en el verdor del aire
La gente grita ¡Hola! ten cuidado
quédate en la acera.

El viento refresca mis brazos
y piernas.
Me siento libre.

Lori Marie Carlson

Las canciones de mi abuela

compartían
el ritmo
de la lavadora

transformaban
la cocina
en una pista de baile

consolaban
las sillas
patas arriba

alegraban
los retratos colgados
de la familia

arrullaban
las sábanas
en el tendedero

les daban sabor
a los frijoles
de olla

las canciones
que cantaba
mi abuela

eran capaces
de hacer salir
a las estrellas

convertir
a mi abuela
en una joven

que de nuevo
iba por agua
al río

y hacerla
reír y llorar
a la vez

My Grandma's Songs

would follow
the beat of
the washing machine

turning
our kitchen
into a dance floor

consoling
the chairs placed
upside down

delighting
the family portraits
on the walls

putting to sleep
the sheets
on the clothesline

giving flavor
to the boiling pot
of beans

the songs
my grandma
used to sing

could make
the stars
come out

could turn
my grandma
into a young girl

going back
to the river
for water

and make her
laugh and cry
at the same time

Francisco X. Alarcón

337

A Persuasive Essay

The purpose of a persuasive essay is to convince someone to think or act in a certain way. Use this student's writing as a model when you write a persuasive essay of your own.

A persuasive essay states a **goal** and gives **reasons**.

Working Together

I think that teamwork is important because it helps you learn more, it helps you make better choices at school, and it helps you make friends.

Teamwork helps you learn more because if you don't know something, you can learn it from your friends. One time at school, I didn't know how to do a map project. It was very hard. My friend Javier knew how to do the project, and he taught me how. We worked as a team. If you do this, you can help somebody learn something that they didn't know.

It's important to support your reasons with **facts** and **examples**.

Another reason teamwork is important is because it helps you make better choices at school. Your friends on the team help you listen to the teacher. They tell you not to do something dangerous. One time a girl in our class wasn't following the rules, and I helped her by showing her what the rules were and why they were important.

The last reason that teamwork is important is that it helps you to make friends by working together. When you work on a team you learn about the other people on your team. You learn to talk with them and solve problems together.

I feel that everyone should work on a team because it teaches you to make good choices, it helps you to learn more than if you worked by yourself, and it helps you to make new friends. Working on a team is also lots of fun.

> Each fact and example needs a paragraph of its own.

> The **ending** sums up a persuasive essay.

Meet the Author

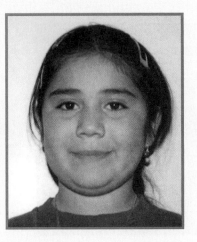

Nancy A.
Grade: three
State: Michigan
Hobbies: writing stories and using the computer
What she wants to be when she grows up: a teacher

Sewing Clothes

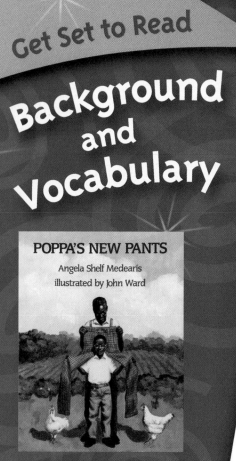

POPPA'S NEW PANTS

Angela Shelf Medearis
illustrated by John Ward

Poppa's New Pants

**Read to find
the meanings
of these words.**

e Glossary

fabric

hem

mended

patterns

plaid

Have you ever ripped your shirt by accident
or had a pair of pants that was too long?
If you have, then you probably know what it's
like to have your clothes **mended**. After you
have mended your clothes, they'll fit well
and you'll look great.

To fix a hole, you
often have to find
another piece of
fabric. Then you
must sew a patch
of the fabric
over the hole.

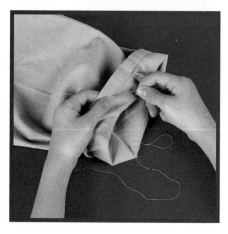

For clothes that
are too long, like
the pants in the
story you are
about to read,
you'll need to **hem**
the fabric. Fold the
fabric under and
sew it in place.

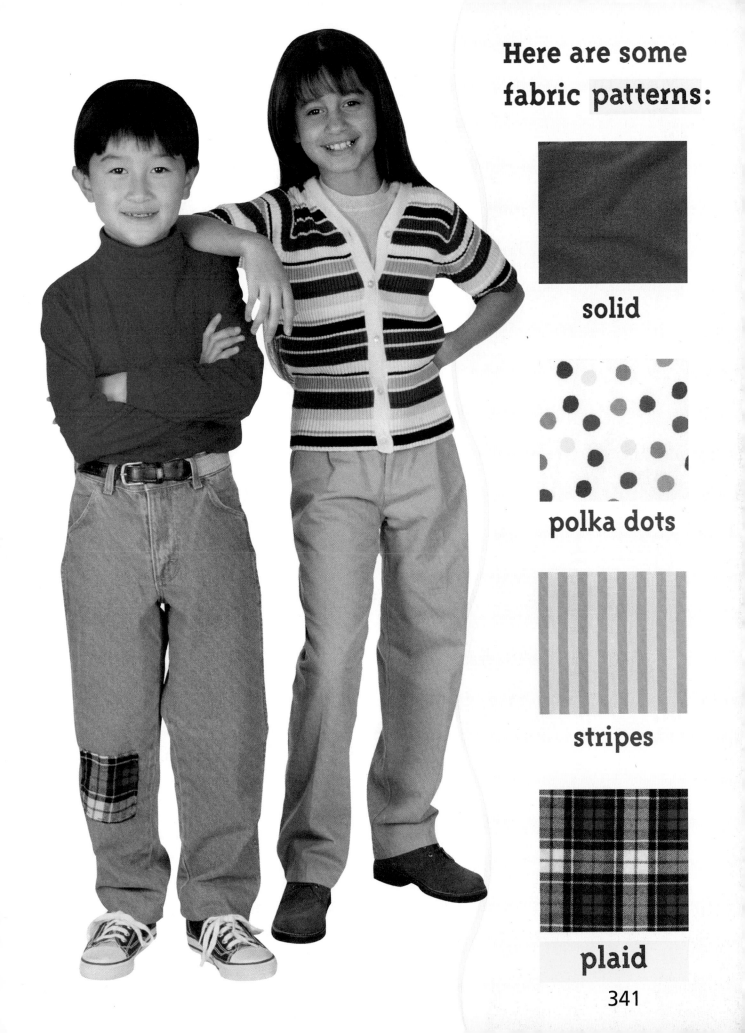

Here are some
fabric patterns:

solid

polka dots

stripes

plaid

Meet the Author
Angela Shelf Medearis

Where she lives: Austin, Texas

Fun fact: One day she started counting all the picture books she owns. She counted 500 and had to stop because she was too tired!

Her books: She writes funny stories because she thinks laughter is one of the happiest sounds in the world.

Other books: *Annie's Gifts*, *Too Much Talk*, *Princess of the Press*, *The Singing Man*

Meet the Illustrator
John Ward

Where he lives: He lives in Freeport, New York, with his wife, Olympia, and his cat, Pumpkin.

Fun fact: He teamed up with Angela Shelf Medearis once again to create *Poppa's Itchy Christmas*, another funny story starring the characters in *Poppa's New Pants*.

Other books: *Fireflies for Nathan* (by Shulamith Levey Oppenheim), *The Bus Ride* (by William Miller)

Internet

Stop by Education Place to learn more about Angela Shelf Medearis and John Ward. **www.eduplace.com/kids**

POPPA'S NEW PANTS

Angela Shelf Medearis

illustrated by John Ward

Strategy Focus

When Poppa buys new pants, his whole family gets involved. As you read, use what you find out about the characters to **predict** what will happen next.

The house was in an uproar. Grandma Tiny had been tearing around all morning like a Texas tornado. Big Mama and Aunt Viney were coming for a visit. Grandma Tiny wanted everything and everyone to look nice when her mother and sister arrived. Poppa and I had beaten so many rugs, washed so many windows, and moved around so much furniture that we'd sweated a bucketful.

We were both glad when Grandma Tiny told us to hitch up old Buck and go to the store.

"Howdy, Poppa. Howdy, George," said Mr. Owens, the storekeeper, when we arrived. "What can I do for y'all today?"

"I've got a list of things to get for Tiny," said Poppa. "Her mama and sister are coming up from Kansas City. She's about to bust a gusset making sure everything's just right."

Mr. Owens laughed as Poppa handed him the list. Poppa and I wandered around the store while Mr. Owens filled our order. We were having a good time looking at the shiny new farm equipment when Poppa spied a pile of pants stacked on a table. Most of them were plain black or brown corduroy.

"Mighty poor pickings here," Poppa said. But when he reached the bottom of the pile, he let out a long whistle.

"George," he said, holding up a pair for me to see. "What do you think about these?"

They were gray pants with a red plaid pattern. The fabric was as velvety soft as old Buck's nose.

"They look real nice, Poppa," I said, "but they must have been made for a giant! They're way too long for you."

Poppa held the pants against his waist. The extra fabric was so long, it draped onto the floor.

"Well," said Poppa, "so they are. But I bet your Grandma Tiny could hem them before church in the morning."

Poppa winked at me and added the long-legged pants to the pile of things we were buying for Grandma Tiny. I winked back and picked out the fattest peppermint stick I could find. Poppa took out his worn leather wallet and paid for everything.

Big Mama and Aunt Viney had arrived by the time we got home. They must have been mighty glad to see me because they snatched me from the wagon like I was a rag doll. Big Mama hugged me so hard that she squeezed the breath right out of my body. Then Aunt Viney and Big Mama took turns covering my face with red lipstick. I almost drowned in a sea of sloppy wet kisses.

"Come on in, y'all," Grandma Tiny finally said. "Supper's just about ready."

Grandma hustled Poppa inside so she could get the groceries put away. I ran after them as fast as I could.

Poppa set down a bag of groceries and unwrapped his new pants. He proudly stretched them across the table for Grandma Tiny, Big Mama, and Aunt Viney to see.

"Nice fabric," said Big Mama.

"What a beautiful pattern," said Aunt Viney.

"Yes, they're mighty pretty pants," said Grandma Tiny. "But they're way yonder too big for a tee-ninchy little man like you, Poppa. Looky here! They're almost long enough to use as a tablecloth."

"Well, honey," said Poppa, "I was hoping you could cut off about six inches and hem them tonight so I could wear them to church tomorrow."

"Oh, honey," said Grandma Tiny, "I'm plum worn out! I've been cooking and cleaning since sunrise. As soon as supper's finished and Mama and Viney get settled in, I'm going to bed!"

"Okay," said Poppa. He turned to Aunt Viney. "Do you think you could hem my pants for me, Viney?"

"Oh Brother-in-law, dear," Aunt Viney said, "I'd love to, really I would, but my eyes are troubling me from driving so long. I need to get some sleep."

"I understand," Poppa said. He looked hopefully at Big Mama and held up his new pants.

"Sorry, son," Big Mama said. "I've got arthritis in my knee joints so bad I can hardly move. I'm looking forward to just resting this evening."

"That's all right, y'all," Poppa said sadly. He put his new pants across the rocker to be mended. Then he went out on the back porch to wash up for supper.

Grandma Tiny called everyone to dinner. She'd cooked everything from chicken and dressing to chocolate cake. The table looked like it was going to buckle in the middle. Supper was delicious, but we were all so tired, conversation was mighty poor. As soon as Poppa was finished eating, he said good night all around and got ready for bed.

Grandma Tiny, Big Mama, and Aunt Viney usually have a good long gossip spell when they get together. But this time, the three women quietly finished their chores and turned in for the night. Big Mama and Aunt Viney had taken over my room. Grandma Tiny made a pallet for me on the kitchen floor while I changed into my pajamas. I took my glasses off and put them on the kitchen table.

I kicked the covers around until I found a soft spot to snuggle into. I could hear Poppa snoring gently and the dark house moaning softly as everyone settled down for the night.

I wasn't used to sleeping in the kitchen. It was kind of spooky. The huge wooden china cabinet and big, black woodburning stove crouched in the corners. The grandfather clock wheezed awake every hour and rang out the time. After awhile, the moon crept into the room, making a big pool of bright, white light by the rocking chair. I jumped when a tree limb scraped against the window screen. I was just drifting off to sleep when I spotted something out of the corner of my eye.

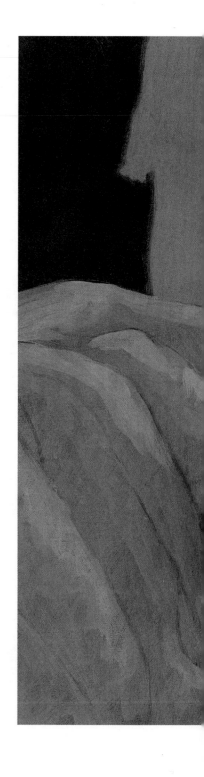

A small, white shape was moving slowly into the kitchen. I was so scared that at first, I forgot to breathe. I squeezed my eyes closed and pulled the covers over my head.

I told myself over and over that there were no such things as ghosts. But I didn't believe it. I could hear whatever it was slowly coming closer . . . and closer . . . and closer. It must have brushed up against the rocking chair because the chair creaked softly back and forth, back and forth. I held my breath until I thought I'd burst. I heard a snip, snip, snip and a funny rustling. Then all was quiet.

It was too quiet! After an hour that seemed like days, I pulled the covers off my head. I finally made my eyes open so I could peek over the edge of the quilt. The ghost-thing was gone! I was tempted to go and sleep on the floor by Poppa and Grandma Tiny.

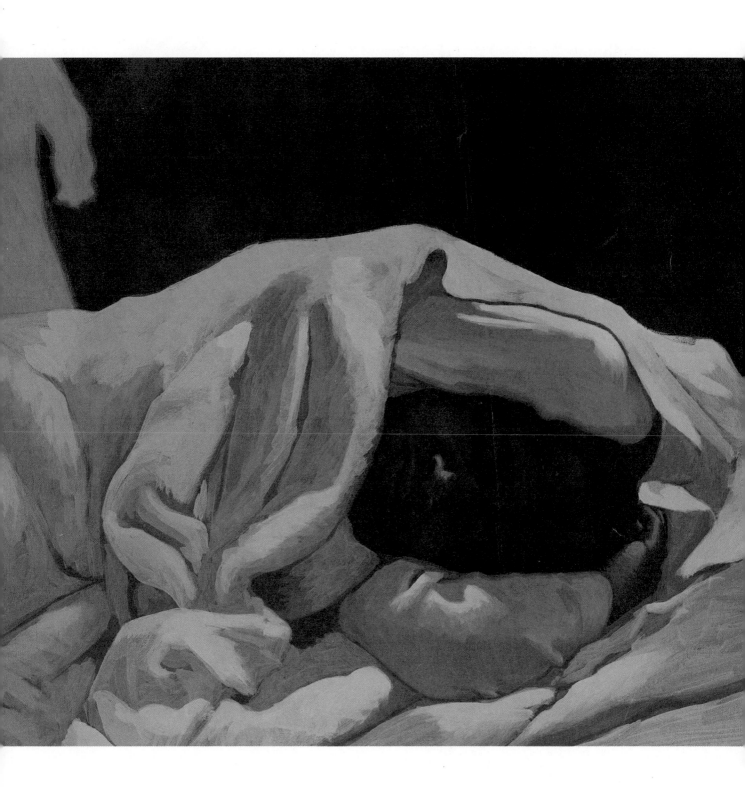

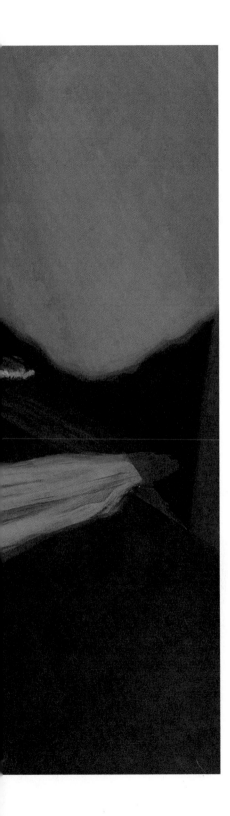

I lay quietly for awhile, mustering up my courage. Just when I thought it was safe to make a run for it, I spied a tall, thin, ghostly white figure drifting into the room. I threw the covers back over my head. My heart was thumping like old Buck's after a long, hard run. I heard the rocking chair creak back and forth, back and forth. Then I heard that funny snip, snip, snip, rustle, rustle sound. After awhile, all was quiet again.

I gave up on the idea of going into Poppa and Grandma Tiny's room. I kept the covers over my head and prayed for morning to come. I must have dozed off because when I opened my eyes, I couldn't figure out where I was. It was so hot, I started to throw the quilt off my head, but then I remembered about the ghosts.

I pulled the covers down inch by inch. I pried open my eyes and slowly looked around the room. A big, white ghost was drifting through the doorway, and it was coming toward me!

I dove down to the foot of the pallet and curled up into a ball. I was shaking all over like a wet dog. I felt something brush past me heavily. Then the rocking chair moaned loudly as it creaked back and forth, back and forth. I heard that snip, snip, snip, rustle, rustle sound and all was quiet again. My teeth were rattling so loud, I thought some of them were going to fall out! I stayed balled up under those blankets like an armadillo for the rest of the night.

"George! George!" The sound of Grandma Tiny's voice woke me the next morning as she whipped the covers off my head.

"Boy, why in the world are you sleeping under all those blankets as hot as it is?" Before I could answer she said, "Go get washed up. We need to hurry if we're going to make it to church on time."

Bright yellow sunlight filled the room. It was morning and I was still alive. I checked to make sure all my limbs were in place. Everything was where it should be. I put on my glasses and stumbled sleepily through the door. Poppa was already on the back porch shaving. I didn't want to say anything about last night. Three ghosts in one evening! I'd never heard a story like that! Besides, maybe I was dreaming. The rocking chair and everything else in the room looked just like they always did.

I mumbled good morning to Poppa and splashed cold water on my face. I'd just finished brushing my teeth when Grandma Tiny came out on the porch.

"Poppa," she said, "hurry up and come inside. There's a surprise for you!" As Poppa went into the kitchen, I followed behind, wondering what all the fuss was about.

Grandma Tiny, Big Mama, and Aunt Viney were gathered around the table. I said good morning and quickly sat down. I didn't want to give Big Mama and Aunt Viney a chance to hug and kiss the life out of me again. Besides, I had had a hard time getting that red lipstick off my face. Grandma Tiny was smiling fit to beat the band. She had Poppa's new pants folded across her arm.

"Honey," said Grandma Tiny, "I got to thinking about what a wonderful husband you are and about how much you wanted to wear these pants. So I got up last night, cut off six inches, and hemmed them for you."

Poppa's smile lit up the room.

"Oh no," said Aunt Viney. "I got to thinking about what a sweet brother-in-law he is, so I got up last night, cut off six inches, and hemmed them up, too!" Poppa stopped smiling and looked at Aunt Viney.

"Well sir, would you listen to this," said Big Mama. "I couldn't rest for thinking about what a good son-in-law he is. So I got up last night, cut six inches off those pants, and hemmed them up, too!"

My mouth dropped open. So these were the ghosts that were haunting me last night!

Poppa grabbed his new pants from Grandma Tiny and held them up to his waist. The beautiful, soft gray pants with the red plaid gently unfolded to his knees.

We all stared at what was left of Poppa's new pants. Poppa hung his head and clutched the pants to his chest. His thin shoulders started to shake. Then all of a sudden, Poppa burst out laughing.

"Well, these pants aren't too long now!" he said.

He put them on and smiled at us. Then he danced around the room in the cut-off pants. He looked so funny we couldn't help laughing. After a long while he wheezed to a stop. Grandma Tiny hugged Poppa around the waist.

"Honey," said Grandma Tiny gently, "don't you worry about those old pants. Next time we go to the store, I'll help you pick out some pants that fit." Poppa hugged her back.

"Come on, y'all," said Big Mama, looking at the clock. "We'll miss Sunday School but we can still make it to church." We scurried around getting ready.

We pulled up in front of Rock Hill Church just in time for the eleven o'clock service. Grandma Tiny, Aunt Viney, and Big Mama looked real pretty in their Sunday going-to-meeting hats. They rustled through the wooden doors of the sanctuary like walking flower gardens. Poppa looked nice too, although he was wearing the same black pants he wears every Sunday. And I must say, I looked mighty sharp in my brand new gray knickers with the red plaid.

The "ghosts" had hemmed them too short for Poppa,
but they were just right for me.

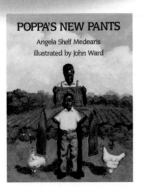

POPPA'S NEW PANTS
Angela Shelf Medearis
illustrated by John Ward

Think About the Selection

1. Why isn't Poppa angry that his pants are now too short for him?

2. George wears glasses. How does this affect what happens in the story?

3. What clues do the author and illustrator give about what really happens during George's restless night?

4. How do you think George could have figured out who the mysterious night visitors were?

5. How do George, Poppa, and the rest of the family show that they care about each other?

6. **Connecting/Comparing** In both *Pepita Talks Twice* and *Poppa's New Pants*, one problem creates others. Tell how each character's decision affects what happens.

Narrating

Write a Funny Story

What other things could happen to Poppa? Maybe his new shirt needs to be mended or his new shoes are too big. Write your own funny story about Poppa. Think of a smart solution to solve the problem.

Tips
- To begin, make a story map.
- Write a beginning that will make people want to keep reading.
- Give your story a clever title.

Math

Make Poppa's Pants

Cut pants like Poppa's out of butcher paper. They should be 48 inches long from the waist to the hem. Then, using information from the story, mark three lines to show where each person hems the pants. Measure carefully! If you have time, decorate your pants with a plaid design.

Social Studies

Compare Community Stores

In a small group, discuss where you would buy groceries, pants, and farm equipment in your community. If possible, use the alphabetical list in the yellow pages of a phone book to help you. Then talk about how these stores compare to the store that Poppa and George visit.

Internet

Solve a Web Logic Puzzle

Collect clues to help Poppa and George fix another crazy mix-up when you visit Education Place. **www.eduplace.com/kids**

Media Link

Skill: How to Read a Comic Strip

❶ Read the comic strip from left to right.

❷ Read the words inside each speech balloon. The tail of each balloon points to the character who is talking.

❸ Look carefully at the faces and the details in each picture.

❹ Laugh!

No Problem!

Just like in a book, the characters in comic strips sometimes have problems to solve. Whatever the problem is, they're sure to solve it in a creative and silly way. So enjoy these smart solutions that will tickle your funny bone too!

CalviN aNd HobbEs

BY BILL WATTERSON

CalviN aNd HobbEs

BY BILL WATTERSON

Background and Vocabulary

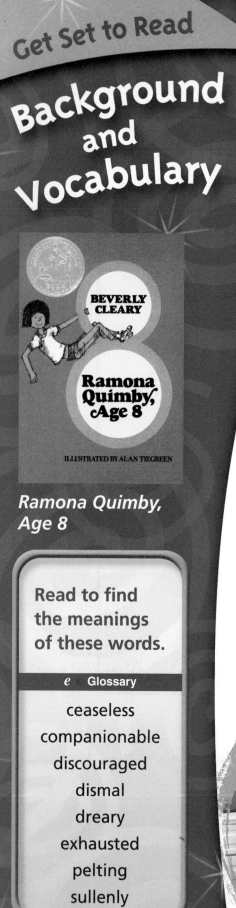

BEVERLY CLEARY

Ramona Quimby, Age 8

ILLUSTRATED BY ALAN TIEGREEN

Ramona Quimby, Age 8

Read to find the meanings of these words.

e ● Glossary

ceaseless
companionable
discouraged
dismal
dreary
exhausted
pelting
sullenly

Rain, Rain, Go Away!

What can you do on a rainy day, when everything outside looks gray and **dreary**? Inside, you can hear the **ceaseless** sound of raindrops **pelting** against the window. Such **dismal** weather can make you feel bored and even sad. Wandering **sullenly** around the house makes you feel **exhausted** and crabby. If you want company but no one else is feeling **companionable**, finding someone to play with or talk to can be hard.

Don't get **discouraged**. Rainy days don't have to be bad days. In the next story, you'll learn what happens when one family spends a cold and rainy Sunday afternoon indoors.

Here are some things you can do for fun on a rainy day.

◀ **Bake some goodies.**

Build a tent and go camping *inside* your house.

◀ **Do an art project you've always wanted to try.**

▶ **Play a favorite game or learn a new one.**

◀ **Read a book!**

Beverly Cleary

One rainy Sunday afternoon, when Beverly Cleary was in third grade, she was feeling bored. She decided to try to read a book. Cleary had never really enjoyed reading before, but this book was so exciting that she couldn't put it down! She read two whole books before bedtime. On that rainy day, Cleary realized that "grown-ups were right after all. Reading was fun!"

Other books: *Ramona's World, Beezus and Ramona, Ramona the Pest, The Mouse and the Motorcycle, Henry and Ribsy*

Alan Tiegreen

Alan Tiegreen has illustrated almost all of Beverly Cleary's books about Ramona Quimby. By now, he feels like the Quimbys are real friends of his. Sitting down to draw them is like inviting them over for a visit. As he starts to draw, he says, "Hey Ramona! Hey Beezus! Good to see you again!"

Internet

Discover more about Beverly Cleary and Alan Tiegreen at Education Place. **www.eduplace.com/kids**

BEVERLY CLEARY

Ramona Quimby, Age 8

ILLUSTRATED BY ALAN TIEGREEN

Strategy Focus

As you read, **summarize** how Ramona feels at the beginning of the rainy Sunday and how her feelings change during the day.

Rainy Sunday

Rainy Sunday afternoons in November were always dismal, but Ramona felt this Sunday was the most dismal of all. She pressed her nose against the living-room window, watching the ceaseless rain pelting down as bare black branches clawed at the electric wires in front of the house. Even lunch, leftovers Mrs. Quimby had wanted to clear out of the refrigerator, had been dreary, with her parents, who seemed tired or discouraged or both, having little to say and Beezus mysteriously moody. Ramona longed for sunshine, sidewalks dry enough for roller-skating, a smiling, happy family.

"Ramona, you haven't cleaned up your room this weekend," said Mrs. Quimby, who was sitting on the couch, sorting through a stack of bills. "And don't press your nose against the window. It leaves a smudge."

Ramona felt as if everything she did was wrong. The whole family seemed cross today, even Picky-picky who meowed at the front door. With a sigh, Mrs. Quimby got up to let him out. Beezus, carrying a towel and shampoo, stalked through the living room into the kitchen, where she began to wash her hair at the sink. Mr. Quimby, studying at the dining-room table as usual, made his pencil scratch angrily across a pad of paper. The television set sat blank and mute, and in the fireplace a log sullenly refused to burn.

Mrs. Quimby sat down and then got up again as Picky-picky, indignant at the wet world outdoors, yowled to come in. "Ramona, clean up your room," she ordered, as she let the cat and a gust of cold air into the house.

"Beezus hasn't cleaned up her room." Ramona could not resist pointing this omission out to her mother.

"I'm not talking about Beezus," said Mrs. Quimby. "I'm talking about you."

Still Ramona did not move from the window. Cleaning up her room seemed such a boring thing to do, no fun at all on a rainy afternoon. She thought vaguely of all the exciting things she would like to do — learn to twirl a lariat, play a musical saw, flip around and over bars in a gymnastic competition while crowds cheered.

"Ramona, *clean up your room*!" Mrs. Quimby raised her voice.

"Well, you don't have to yell at me." Ramona's feelings were hurt by the tone of her mother's voice. The log in the fireplace settled, sending a puff of smoke into the living room.

"Then do it," snapped Mrs. Quimby. "Your room is a disaster area."

Mr. Quimby threw down his pencil. "Young lady, you do what your mother says, and you do it now. She shouldn't have to tell you three times."

"Well, all right, but you don't have to be so cross," said Ramona. To herself she thought, Nag, nag, nag.

Sulkily Ramona took her hurt feelings off to her room, where she pulled a week's collection of dirty socks from under her bed. On her way to the bathroom hamper, she looked down the hall and saw her sister standing in the living room, rubbing her hair with a towel.

"Mother, I think you're mean," said Beezus from under the towel.

Ramona stopped to listen.

"I don't care how mean you think I am," answered
Mrs. Quimby. "You are not going to go, and that is that."

"But all the other girls are going," protested Beezus.

"I don't care if they are," said Mrs. Quimby. "You are not."

Ramona heard the sound of a pencil being slammed on the
table and her father saying, "Your mother is right. Now would
you kindly give me a little peace and quiet so I can get on with
my work."

Beezus flounced past Ramona into her room and slammed
the door. Sobs were heard, loud, angry sobs.

Where can't she go? Ramona wondered, as she dumped her
socks into the hamper. Then, because she had been so good
about picking up her room, Ramona returned to the living room,
where Picky-picky, as cross and bored as the rest of the family, was
once again meowing at the front door. "Where can't Beezus go?"
she asked.

Mrs. Quimby opened the front door, and when Picky-picky hesitated, vexed by the cold wind that swept into the room, assisted him out with her toe. "She can't sleep over at Mary Jane's house with a bunch of girls from her class."

A year ago Ramona would have agreed with her mother so that her mother would love her more than Beezus, but this year she knew that she too might want to spend the night at someone's house someday. "Why can't Beezus sleep at Mary Jane's?" she asked.

"Because she comes home exhausted and grouchy." Mrs. Quimby stood by the door, waiting. Picky-picky's yowl was twisted by the wind, and when she opened the door, another cold gust swept through the house.

"With the price of fuel oil being what it is, we can't afford to let the cat out," remarked Mr. Quimby.

"Would you like to take the responsibility if I don't let him out?" asked Mrs. Quimby, before she continued with her answer to Ramona. "There are four people in the family, and she has no right to make the whole day disagreeable for the rest of us because she has been up half the night giggling with a bunch of silly girls. Besides, a growing girl needs her rest."

Ramona silently agreed with her mother about Beezus'
coming home cross after such a party. At the same time, she
wanted to make things easier for herself when she was in
junior high school. "Maybe this time they would go to sleep
earlier," she suggested.

"Fat chance," said Mrs. Quimby, who rarely spoke so
rudely. "And furthermore, Ramona, Mrs. Kemp did not come
right out and say so, but she did drop a hint that you are not
playing as nicely with Willa Jean as you might."

Ramona heaved a sigh that seemed to come from the
soles of her feet. In the bedroom, Beezus, who had run out
of real sobs, was working hard to force out fake sobs to show
her parents how mean they were to her.

Mrs. Quimby ignored the sighs and the sobs and
continued. "Ramona, you know that getting along at the
Kemps' is your job in this family. I've told you that before."

How could Ramona explain to her mother that Willa Jean
had finally caught on that Sustained Silent Reading was just
plain reading a book? For a while, Willa Jean wanted Ramona
to read aloud a few boring books the Kemps owned, the sort
of books people who did not know anything about children
so often gave them. Willa Jean listened to them several
times, grew bored, and now insisted on playing beauty shop.
Ramona did not want her fingernails painted by Willa Jean
and knew she would be blamed if Willa Jean spilled nail polish.
Instead of Mrs. Kemp's taking care of Ramona, Ramona was
taking care of Willa Jean.

Ramona looked at the carpet, sighed again, and said,
"I try." She felt sorry for herself, misunderstood and
unappreciated. Nobody in the whole world understood
how hard it was to go to the Kemps' house after school
when she did not have a bicycle.

Mrs. Quimby relented. "I know it isn't easy," she said with a half smile, "but don't give up." She gathered up the bills and checkbook and went into the kitchen, where she began to write checks at the kitchen table.

Ramona wandered into the dining room to seek comfort from her father. She laid her cheek against the sleeve of his plaid shirt and asked, "Daddy, what are you studying?"

Once again Mr. Quimby threw down his pencil. "I am studying the cognitive processes of children," he answered.

Ramona raised her head to look at him. "What does that mean?" she asked.

"How kids think," her father told her.

Ramona did not like the sound of this subject at all. "Why are you studying *that*?" she demanded. Some things should be private, and how children thought was one of them. She did not like the idea of grown-ups snooping around in thick books trying to find out.

"That is exactly what I have been asking myself." Mr. Quimby was serious. "Why am I studying this stuff when we have bills to pay?"

"Well, I don't think you should," said Ramona. "It's none of your business how kids think." Then she quickly added, because she did not want her father to drop out of school and be a checker again, "There are lots of other things you could study. Things like fruit flies."

Mr. Quimby smiled at Ramona and rumpled her hair. "I doubt if anyone could figure out how you think," he said, which made Ramona feel better, as if her secret thoughts were still safe.

Mr. Quimby sat gnawing his pencil and staring out the window at the rain. Beezus, who had run out of fake sobs, emerged from her room, red-eyed and damp-haired, to stalk about the house not speaking to anyone.

Ramona flopped down on the couch. She hated rainy Sundays, especially this one, and longed for Monday when she could escape to school. The Quimbys' house seemed to have grown smaller during the day until it was no longer big enough to hold her family and all its problems. She tried not to think of the half-overheard conversations of her parents after the girls had gone to bed, grown-up talk that Ramona understood just enough to know her parents were concerned about their future.

Ramona had deep, secret worries of her own. She worried that her father might accidentally be locked in the frozen-food warehouse, where it was so cold it sometimes snowed indoors. What if he was filling a big order, and the men who were lucky enough to get small orders to fill left work ahead of him and forgot and locked the warehouse, and he couldn't get out and froze to death? Of course that wouldn't happen. "But it might," insisted a tiny voice in the back of her mind. Don't be silly, she told the little voice. "Yes, but —" began the little voice. And despite the worry that would not go away Ramona wanted her father to go on working so he could stay in school and someday get a job he liked.

   While Ramona worried, the house was silent except for the sound of rain and the scratch of her father's pencil. The smoking log settled in the fireplace, sending up a few feeble sparks. The day grew darker, Ramona was beginning to feel hungry, but there was no comfortable bustle of cooking in the kitchen.

   Suddenly Mr. Quimby slammed shut his book and threw down his pencil so hard it bounced onto the floor. Ramona sat up. Now what was wrong?

   "Come on, everybody," said her father. "Get cleaned up. Let's stop this grumping around. We are going out for dinner, and we are going to smile and be pleasant if it kills us. That's an order!"

The girls stared at their father and then at one another. What was going on? They had not gone out to dinner for months, so how could they afford to go now?

"To the Whopperburger?" asked Ramona.

"Sure," said Mr. Quimby, who appeared cheerful for the first time that day. "Why not? The sky's the limit."

Mrs. Quimby came into the living room with a handful of stamped envelopes. "But Bob —" she began.

"Now don't worry," her husband said. "We'll manage. During Thanksgiving I'll be putting in more hours in the warehouse and getting more overtime. There's no reason why we can't have a treat once in a while. And the Whopperburger isn't exactly your four-star gourmet restaurant."

Ramona was afraid her mother might give a lecture on the evils of junk food, but she did not. Gloom and anger were forgotten. Clothes were changed, hair combed, Picky-picky was shut in the basement, and the family was on its way in the old car with the new transmission that never balked at backing down the driveway. Off the Quimbys sped to the nearest Whopperburger, where they discovered other families must have wanted to get out of the house on a rainy day, for the restaurant was crowded, and they had to wait for a table.

There were enough chairs for the grown-ups and Beezus, but Ramona, who had the youngest legs, had to stand up. She amused herself by punching the buttons on the vending machine in time to the Muzak, which was playing "Tie a Yellow Ribbon 'Round the Old Oak Tree." She even danced a little to the music, and, when the tune came to an end, she turned around and found herself face to face with an old man with neatly trimmed gray hair and a moustache that turned up at the ends. He was dressed as if everything he wore — a flowered shirt, striped tie, tweed coat and plaid slacks — had come from different stores or from a rummage sale, except that the crease in his trousers was sharp and his shoes were shined.

The old man, whose back was very straight, saluted Ramona as if she were a soldier and said, "Well, young lady, have you been good to your mother?"

Ramona was stunned. She felt her face turn red to the tips of her ears. She did not know how to answer such a question. Had she been good to her mother? Well . . . not always, but why was this stranger asking? It was none of his business. He had no right to ask such a question.

Ramona looked to her parents for help and discovered they were waiting with amusement for her answer. So were the rest of the people who were waiting for tables. Ramona scowled at the man. She did not have to answer him if she did not want to.

The hostess saved Ramona by calling out, "Quimby, party of four," and leading the family to a plastic-upholstered booth.

"Why didn't you answer the man?" Beezus was as amused as everyone else.

"I'm not supposed to talk to strangers," was Ramona's dignified answer.

"But Mother and Daddy are with us," Beezus pointed out, rather meanly, Ramona thought.

"Remember," said Mr. Quimby, as he opened his menu, "we are all going to smile and enjoy ourselves if it kills us."

As Ramona picked up her menu, she was still seething inside. Maybe she hadn't always been good to her mother, but that man had no right to pry. When she discovered he was seated in a single booth across the aisle, she gave him an indignant look, which he answered with a merry wink. So he had been teasing. Well, Ramona didn't like it.

When Ramona opened her menu, she made an exciting discovery. She no longer had to depend on colored pictures of hamburgers, French fries, chili, and steak to help her make up her mind. She could now read what was offered. She studied carefully, and when she came to the bottom of the menu, she read the dreaded words, "Child's Plate for Children Under Twelve." Then came the list of choices: fish sticks, chicken drumsticks, hot dogs. None of them, to Ramona, food for a treat. They were food for a school cafeteria.

"Daddy," Ramona whispered, "do I have to have a child's plate?"

"Not if you don't want to." Her father's smile was understanding. Ramona ordered the smallest adult item on the menu.

Whopperburger was noted for fast service, and in a few minutes the waitress set down the Quimbys' dinners: a hamburger and French fries for Ramona, a cheeseburger and French fries for Beezus and her mother, and hamburgers with chili for her father.

Ramona bit into her hamburger. Bliss. Warm, soft, juicy, tart with relish. Juice dribbled down her chin. She noticed her mother start to say something and change her mind. Ramona caught the dribble with her paper napkin before it reached her collar. The French fries — crisp on the outside, mealy on the inside — tasted better than anything Ramona had ever eaten.

The family ate in companionable silence for a few moments until the edge was taken off their hunger. "A little change once in a while does make a difference," said Mrs. Quimby. "It does us all good."

"Especially after the way —" Ramona stopped herself from finishing with, "— after the way Beezus acted this afternoon." Instead she sat up straight and smiled.

"Well, I wasn't the only one who —" Beezus also stopped in midsentence and smiled. The parents looked stern, but they managed to smile. Suddenly everyone relaxed and laughed.

The old man, Ramona noticed, was eating a steak. She wished her father could afford a steak.

As much as she enjoyed her hamburger, Ramona was unable to finish. It was too much. She was happy when her mother did not say, "Someone's eyes are bigger than her stomach." Her father, without commenting on the unfinished hamburger, included her in the orders of apple pie with hot cinnamon sauce and ice cream.

Ramona ate what she could, and after watching the ice cream melt into the cinnamon sauce, she glanced over at the old man, who was having a serious discussion with the waitress. She seemed surprised and upset about something. The Muzak, conversation of other customers, and rattle of dishes made eavesdropping impossible. The waitress left. Ramona saw

her speak to the manager, who listened and then nodded. For a moment Ramona thought the man might not have enough money to pay for the steak he had eaten. Apparently he did, however, for after listening to what the waitress had to say, he left a tip under the edge of his plate and picked up his check. To Ramona's embarrassment, he stood up, winked, and saluted her again. Then he left. Ramona did not know what to make of him.

She turned back to her family, whose smiles were now genuine rather than determined. The sight of them gave her courage to ask the question that had been nibbling at the back of her mind, "Daddy, you aren't going to be a college dropout, are you?"

Mr. Quimby finished a mouthful of pie before he answered, "Nope."

Ramona wanted to make sure. "And you won't ever be a checker and come home cross again?"

"Well," said her father, "I can't promise I won't come home cross, but if I do, it won't be from standing at the cash register trying to remember forty-two price changes in the produce section while a long line of customers, all in a hurry, wait to pay for their groceries."

Ramona was reassured.

When the waitress descended on the Quimbys to offer the grown-ups a second cup of coffee, Mr. Quimby said, "Check, please."

The waitress looked embarrassed. "Well . . . a . . ." She hesitated. "This has never happened before, but your meals have already been paid for."

The Quimbys looked at her in astonishment. "But who paid for them?" demanded Mr. Quimby.

"A lonely gentleman who left a little while ago," answered the waitress.

"He must have been the man who sat across the aisle," said Mrs. Quimby. "But why would he pay for our dinners? We never saw him before in our lives."

The waitress smiled. "Because he said you are such a nice family, and because he misses his children and grandchildren." She dashed off with her pot of coffee, leaving the Quimbys in

surprised, even shocked, silence. A nice family? After the way they had behaved on a rainy Sunday.

"A mysterious stranger just like in a book," said Beezus. "I never thought I'd meet one."

"Poor lonely man," said Mrs. Quimby at last, as Mr. Quimby shoved a tip under his saucer. Still stunned into silence, the family struggled into their wraps and splashed across the parking lot to their car, which started promptly and backed obediently out of its parking space. As the windshield wipers began their rhythmic exercise, the family rode in silence, each thinking of the events of the day.

"You know," said Mrs. Quimby thoughtfully, as the car left the parking lot and headed down the street, "I think he was right. We are a nice family."

"Not all the time," said Ramona, as usual demanding accuracy.

"Nobody is nice all the time," answered her father. "Or if they are, they are boring."

"Not even your parents are nice all the time," added Mrs. Quimby.

Ramona secretly agreed, but she had not expected her parents to admit it. Deep down inside, she felt she herself was nice all the time, but sometimes on the outside her niceness sort of — well, curdled. Then people did not understand how nice she really was. Maybe other people curdled too.

"We have our ups and downs," said Mrs. Quimby, "but we manage to get along, and we stick together."

"We are nicer than some families I know," said Beezus. "Some families don't even eat dinner together." After a moment she made a confession. "I don't really like sleeping on someone's floor in a sleeping bag."

"I didn't think you did." Mrs. Quimby reached back and patted Beezus on the knee. "That's one reason I said you couldn't go. You didn't want to go, but didn't want to admit it."

Ramona snuggled inside her car coat, feeling cozy enclosed in the car with the heater breathing warm air on her nice family. She was a member of a nice sticking-together family, and she was old enough to be depended upon, so she could ignore — or at least try to ignore — a lot of things. Willa Jean — she would try reading her Sustained Silent Reading books aloud because Willa Jean was old enough to

understand most of them. That should work for a little while.
Mrs. Whaley — some things were nice about her and some
were not. Ramona could get along.

"That man paying for our dinner was sort of like a happy
ending," remarked Beezus, as the family, snug in their car,
drove through the rain and the dark toward Klickitat Street.

"A happy ending for today," corrected Ramona.
Tomorrow they would begin all over again.

Think About the Selection

1. Why does Mr. Quimby decide that the family needs to go out to dinner?

2. How does Beverly Cleary make Ramona think and act like a real person? Find examples from the story.

3. Do you agree that the Quimbys are a nice family? Explain your answer.

4. Why do you think Ramona feels happier at the end of the story?

5. What does Cleary mean by the last sentence, "Tomorrow they would begin all over again"?

6. **Connecting/Comparing** In each story in this theme, how does a family help each other find a smart solution to a problem?

Write a Thank-You Note

When someone does something kind for you, you should always thank them. Write a thank-you note that Ramona might have written to the man who paid for the Quimbys' dinner.

Tips

- Write the date at the top of the note.
- Begin with a greeting.
- End with a closing and a signature.

Add Up a Restaurant Check

Look on page 387 to find out what kind of hamburger each of the Quimbys ate for dinner. Add up the prices from the menu below.

Bonus Add on four pieces of apple pie, four sodas, and two cups of coffee to find the total cost of the Quimbys' dinner.

Whopperburger Menu	
Hamburger with French fries	$5.75
Cheeseburger with French fries	$6.25
Hamburgers with chili	$7.50
Soda	$1.00
Cup of coffee	$1.25
Apple pie	$2.50

Role-Play Ordering Food

With a partner, take turns playing a customer and a server in a restaurant. When you play the role of the customer, tell the server what you'd like to eat and drink. When you play the role of the server, listen carefully and write down the order. For fun, make up a menu for the customer to use.

Tips

- The server should start by asking, "May I take your order?"
- Speak clearly and be polite to one another.

Take an Online Poll

Ramona loves her Whopperburger dinner. If you could pick your perfect meal, what would it be? Come to Education Place and vote for your food favorites. **www.eduplace.com/kids**

Drama Link

Skill: How to Read a Play

❶ Read the title. Look at the **cast of characters** to learn who is in the play.

❷ Be an actor! Plays are meant to be performed, so take turns reading each character's **lines** aloud.

❸ As you perform, read the **stage directions** to yourself. They describe the setting and the characters' actions.

Henry and Ramona

based on the books by Beverly Cleary
dramatized by Cynthia J. McGean

CAST OF CHARACTERS

HENRY HUGGINS: earnest boy, almost 11 years old

BYRON MURPHY (MURPH): a "boy genius," Henry's age

BEEZUS QUIMBY: girl about Henry's age, Henry's best friend, very practical

RAMONA QUIMBY: Beezus' younger sister, about 5 years old, imaginative and underfoot

Act I, Scene Nine

PLACE: Klickitat Street

(A rainy, cloudy day in early fall. HENRY enters. MURPH enters with a Journal *bag full of papers.)*

MURPH: *(to HENRY)* You can have the route.

HENRY: What?!

MURPH: I said, you can have the route.

HENRY: You mean you don't want it?

MURPH: No.

HENRY: *(suspiciously)* How come?

MURPH: Ramona.

HENRY: Ramona?! She's just a little kid!

MURPH: I know, but she can sure make a lot of trouble.

HENRY: I'm not so sure Mr. Capper wants me to have a route.

MURPH: Yes he does.

HENRY: How do you know?

MURPH: I asked him. *(Pause.)* I guess I shouldn't have taken the route when I knew you wanted it, but I just had to. My other route was too far away, and I needed money to buy parts for Thorvo. Dad thinks my robot's a waste of time, so I have to pay for the parts myself. But Ramona's making so much trouble I prob'ly would've lost the route anyway.

HENRY: Okay, Murph, I'll take the route.

MURPH: *(relieved)* Thanks. Here's the route book and the papers. *(He hands HENRY the* Journal *bag.)*

HENRY: Murph . . . does your dad really think Thorvo's a waste of time?

MURPH: Yeah. I guess I'll have to put all that stuff away 'til I figure out how to pay for parts. *(Pause.)* If you still want to make that private phone line, I have most of the stuff. And I already know how to build one.

HENRY: You do?

MURPH: Sure.

HENRY: Okay.

MURPH: Guess I'll see ya around. Good luck with the route.

HENRY: Thanks. *(MURPH exits.)* Imagine! A genius licked by a five-year-old! She's just a kindergartner. I'm not gonna let her stand in my way! Maybe I'm no genius, but I'm still smarter than a five-year-old.

(HENRY goes to get his bike. RAMONA enters and sits down.)

RAMONA: Hello.

HENRY: Hello, Ramona. *(He begins to deliver papers. RAMONA follows after him, picking up all his papers. HENRY spots her.)* Hey, cut that out! Give me those!

RAMONA: No! I'm going to deliver them!
(She and HENRY have a tug of war. He grabs the papers, and she begins a tantrum. BEEZUS enters.)

BEEZUS: Ramona! You're supposed to be in the house!

RAMONA: *(grabbing HENRY in an attempt to get the papers back)* I'm a paperboy — like Henry and Murph!

HENRY: Get off me, will ya?

BEEZUS: *(prying RAMONA free from HENRY)* I'm sorry, Henry. *(RAMONA is wailing.)* Ramona, be *quiet*!
(To HENRY) Mom says she has to stay in her room 'til the papers are delivered, but she keeps getting out.

HENRY: We've got to do something, or I'll lose my route.

BEEZUS: We've tried, but when we don't want her to do something, she just wants to do it even more. The only way I can ever get her to do what I want is by getting her to pretend . . . wait a minute — !
(BEEZUS and HENRY look at each other and get an idea. They whisper together. RAMONA is now trying to listen in, pleased to be the center of attention.)

HENRY: I know just the thing. Hang on to Ramona, Beezus.

BEEZUS: Gotcha. *(HENRY exits behind his house.)*

RAMONA: Where's Henry going?

BEEZUS: You'll see.

RAMONA: I want to go TOO!

BEEZUS: Ramona, how do you know you want to go if you don't know where he's going?!

RAMONA: But I WANT to go!

BEEZUS: Let's pretend that we're waiting for a bus. When Henry comes back, that means the bus is here. Okay?

RAMONA: Henry's not a bus, he's a paperboy. *(HENRY returns with a big cardboard box made into a makeshift robot head.)*

HENRY: Hey, Ramona — how would you like to be a robot like Thorvo? *(RAMONA nods excitedly.)* Now, remember. A robot can't move very fast, and it jerks along when it walks. *(He places the cardboard box over RAMONA's head.)*

RAMONA: Clank, clank. *(She begins walking, slowly and jerkily, like a robot.)*

BEEZUS: And a robot can't bend at the waist because it doesn't have any waist!

RAMONA: Clank.

BEEZUS: Henry, you're a genius!

HENRY: You're the one who thought of pretending.

BEEZUS: That's true. Well, guess you've got some papers to deliver.

HENRY: Yup. I better get going. *(He begins to leave. RAMONA waves at him as a robot.)*

RAMONA: Clank, clank!

HENRY: Clank, clank, Ramona! *(HENRY exits. RAMONA clanks out with BEEZUS.)*

Check Your Progress

So far in this theme, you have read three selections about solving problems. Now you're going to read and compare two more selections. You will also practice your test-taking skills.

Before you begin, think about Ofelia Dumas Lachtman's letter on pages 299–300. Compare the way that problem is solved with the way the problems in this theme are solved.

Here are two more selections with problems that need solving. As you read, think about what makes each solution a smart one.

Read and Compare

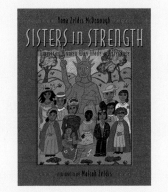

Helen Keller
by Yona Zeldis McDonough

Read about how a blind and deaf girl learns to communicate.

Try these strategies:
Evaluate
Monitor and Clarify

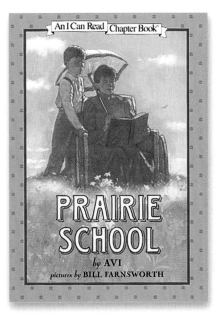

This story is about a boy who thinks reading is not important.

Try these strategies:
Summarize
Predict and Infer

Strategies in Action *Use all your reading strategies while you read.*

HELEN KELLER

by Yona Zeldis McDonough

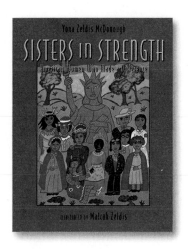

Helen Keller was born in 1880. She was just nineteen months old when she had an illness that changed her life.

Captain Keller and his wife watched as their baby Helen twisted and moaned with fever. Doctors were unable to help, and the Kellers feared she would die. Miraculously, Helen recovered. But she could no longer see or hear, and was condemned to a silent, dark world.

Her early life in Tuscumbia, Alabama, was hard. Although bright, Helen was always frustrated by her condition. She fell or slammed into things when she played or ran. Other children avoided her because she hit them or broke their toys. When she smelled the cake her mother had baked for her sixth birthday, she destroyed it with her hands and stuffed chunks of it into her mouth. Her mother wanted to save the cake for a special supper, so she took it away, but Helen began to sob and kick. When her mother

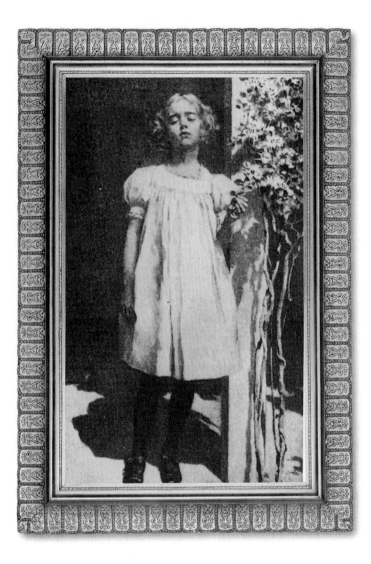

tried to comfort her, Helen rushed outside, right into a thorny bush. The birthday supper was ruined. At that point, the Kellers knew they had to find someone to help their daughter.

Not long after this realization, the Kellers traveled to Washington, D.C., where Helen met Alexander Graham Bell, the inventor of the telephone. Dr. Bell had spent years trying to help deaf people. He took Helen on his lap. She touched his beard and held his pocket watch to her cheek to feel its ticking. Dr. Bell told her parents about a special school for the blind in Boston, where a blind and deaf girl had been taught to communicate. Maybe the school would send a teacher for the Kellers.

Helen was soon startled by the arrival of a young stranger, Anne Sullivan. Anne had been nearly blind before an operation restored her sight. Now she was here to help Helen. She gave Helen a doll and then took her hand and pressed strange and unfamiliar patterns on it with her fingers. Anne was making the letters D-O-L-L. Helen was confused, but soon learned to imitate the patterns. C-A-T was for when they stroked the cat. C-A-K-E meant she wanted a treat and M-I-L-K a drink. But Helen didn't understand that she was spelling words.

Life with "Miss Annie" was a roller-coaster ride. Helen liked the sewing cards and beads Miss Annie gave her, as well as their walks and pony rides in the woods. But Miss Annie was strict. No more roaming around the table, grabbing food. Helen had to sit in her chair, fold her napkin, and eat with a spoon. The rules made Helen angry. She would hit Miss Annie. Helen even locked the teacher in a room and hid the key.

Then one day, they stopped beside the outdoor pump. Helen held her hand under the spout while Annie pumped. Annie took her other hand and spelled W-A-T-E-R. All at once, something in Helen's face changed. She spelled water herself, several times. She pointed down, and Annie spelled out G-R-O-U-N-D. Suddenly, Helen understood that the signs she had been making were words, and words could be attached to objects, people, animals — anything at all! She pointed to Annie, and Annie spelled T-E-A-C-H-E-R, which became her new name.

Helen's world brightened after that day. She went on to learn Braille, a way for blind people to read. She learned how to speak, which took a long time. Later, she graduated from college with high grades. She became an author and a speaker, and spent most of her life helping blind and deaf people throughout the world.

PRAIRIE SCHOOL

by Avi

illustrated by Stacey Schuett

This story takes place in Colorado over one hundred years ago. Noah Bidson, who is nine years old, works hard on the family farm. He loves his chores and the freedom of prairie life. All that changes when his Aunt Dora arrives to teach him how to read. Noah is angry. What use does he have for books?

ONE WEEK

MONDAY

Aunt Dora set up her school in the sod house. A lamp was lit because it was so dim.

But then Noah went to fetch water from the creek two miles away. He took a long time coming back. When he did, Aunt Dora pointed to the letter she had written on the board. "A," she said. "Please repeat that."

"A," Noah said. Then he stood up. "Aunt Dora, I forgot to feed the chickens."

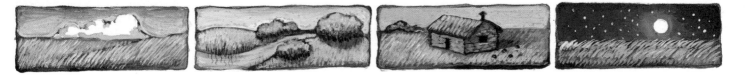

TUESDAY

When Noah came back from his morning chores, he sat in his chair and fidgeted. At the blackboard Aunt Dora wrote the letter B. "This is B," she said. "Can you read it?"

Just then Noah saw a snake in the front yard. "Got to get that snake!" he cried. He didn't come back all day.

WEDNESDAY

Aunt Dora wrote the alphabet on the board. She pointed to the letters with a stick. "Noah, can you find the letters for your name?"

"Nope."

"Noah, don't you ever want to read?"

"Nothing to read on the prairie," he said.

THURSDAY

Whenever Aunt Dora tried to teach, Noah excused himself to do chores. He did them as slowly as possible.

FRIDAY

Aunt Dora put numbers on the board. "Would you like to learn to count?" she asked.

"Aunt Dora," Noah said, "it's too hot and dark to stay in here."

"Noah," Aunt Dora said, "you are as stubborn as a downhill mule on an uphill road."

SATURDAY

Aunt Dora was too upset to do any teaching.

SUNDAY

"I'm afraid my kind of schooling won't work here," Aunt Dora said to her sister and brother-in-law.

"Dora," her sister said kindly, "life out here is different."

"And I'm afraid," said Mr. Bidson, "our Noah has become a regular prairie dog."

Aunt Dora laughed. "Now I know what to do!"

PRAIRIE SCHOOL

The next morning when Noah came back from hauling water, Aunt Dora had wheeled herself out of the sod house. On her lap was a book. "Noah," Aunt Dora said, "push me around. I need to see this prairie of yours."

"The ground isn't flat," he warned. He wondered how her wheelchair would ride.

"Well, then, you'd best tie me in."

When Noah pushed Aunt Dora over the prairie, the chair jumped and rolled like a bucking horse. Aunt Dora held on. "It's very beautiful here," she said. "What is the name of that yellow flower?"

Noah shrugged.

Aunt Dora looked through her book. "It's a dogtooth violet," she said, reading. "The only lily in this area. It grows from a bulb. The Indians boil the bulb and eat it for food."

Noah was surprised. "Is that true?" he asked.

Aunt Dora pointed to the page. "That's what it says here. Now show me some more prairie," she said.

All day Noah wheeled her around. All day Aunt Dora asked questions about what she saw. Noah told her what he knew. Each time, Aunt Dora looked in her book and told him more.

Noah was puzzled. "Aunt Dora, how come you're so smart?"

"I'm just smart enough to read," she said.

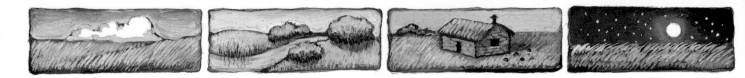

THE STARS

That night Aunt Dora asked Noah to take her outside. The night sky was full of stars. "Noah," Aunt Dora said, "what do you see up there?"

"Stars," he said.

"I see stars too. But I can also see pictures."

"Pictures? Where?"

"There's the mighty warrior Hercules. There is a snake. There's the Big Dipper. Nearby is the Little Dipper."

Noah said, "Are you going to tell me you get all that from a book too?"

"Reading books only helps me understand what I see and hear."

Noah hung his head. "There are no books on the prairie."

"One of my trunks is full of books."

Noah said nothing.

"Noah," Aunt Dora said softly, "learn to read and you'll read the prairie. What do you say to that?"

After a moment Noah said, "I might try."

Think and Compare

Helen Keller
SISTERS in STRENGTH

by Yona Zeldis McDonough

Pepita Talks Twice
Pepita habla dos veces

BY OFELIA DUMAS LACHTMAN

POPPA'S NEW PANTS

Angela Shelf Medearis
illustrated by John Ward

BEVERLY CLEARY

Ramona Quimby, Age 8

ILLUSTRATED BY ALAN TIEGREEN

1. Compare the way Annie Sullivan helps Helen Keller with the way Aunt Dora helps Noah Bidson. How is their help alike and different?

2. Pepita and Noah each learn something important. How do you think their lives will change?

3. George's family had trouble getting Poppa's new pants to fit. How do you think Ramona Quimby's family might have solved the problem?

4. Think about a time you solved a problem. Compare your experience with a character's experience in this theme.

Strategies in Action Which reading strategies helped you the most in this theme? Why?

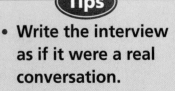

Informing

Write an Interview

Have two characters in the theme interview each other. How did they each solve their problems? Write the interview.

Tips

- Write the interview as if it were a real conversation.
- Put yourself in each character's place as you write the interview.

 # Writing a Story

Some tests may ask you to write a story about a topic, or prompt. A test for *Smart Solutions* might have this prompt.

> Write a story about some students who have a problem at school and what happens when they try to solve it.

1 Read the prompt.

Find the key words that tell the topic and the kind of writing. Say in your own words what you need to do. Decide what to write about.

2 Explore and plan.

Brainstorm characters, events, and details for your story. Think of a problem that one of the characters can solve. Organize your events and details in a chart.

Here is a sample story map.

Characters: Coach Woods, Leah	Setting: P.E. Class
Problem: Leah forgets socks; can't play in P.E.	
Beginning: Leah forgets to put on socks. **Middle:** goes to P.E. class; Coach won't let her play. **End:** Mom puts socks in Leah's backpack.	
Solution: Leah keeps socks in her backpack.	

Write your paper.

Write a draft of your story. Follow the chart you made. Revise your story. Look for places to add exact words and details. Proofread your story to correct errors.

Here is the beginning of a sample story.

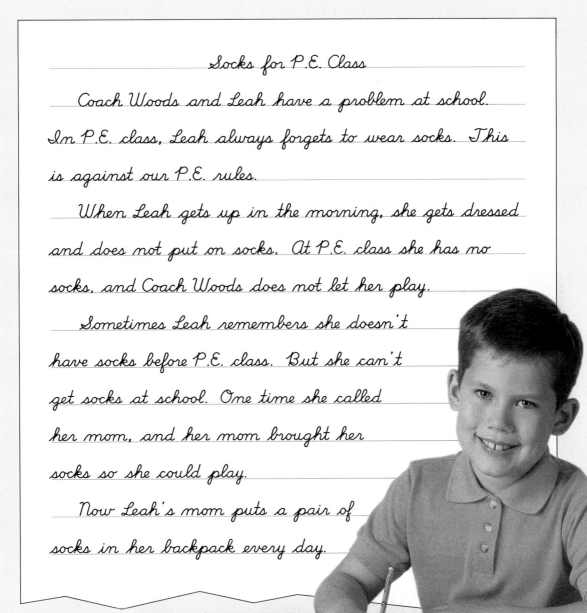

> Socks for P.E. Class
>
> Coach Woods and Leah have a problem at school. In P.E. class, Leah always forgets to wear socks. This is against our P.E. rules.
>
> When Leah gets up in the morning, she gets dressed and does not put on socks. At P.E. class she has no socks, and Coach Woods does not let her play.
>
> Sometimes Leah remembers she doesn't have socks before P.E. class. But she can't get socks at school. One time she called her mom, and her mom brought her socks so she could play.
>
> Now Leah's mom puts a pair of socks in her backpack every day.

This glossary contains meanings and pronunciations for some of the words in this book. The Full Pronunciation Key shows how to pronounce each consonant and vowel in a special spelling. At the bottom of the glossary pages is a shortened form of the full key.

Full Pronunciation Key

Consonant Sounds

b	**bib**, ca**bb**age	kw	**ch**oir, **qu**ick	t	**t**igh**t**, stopp**ed**
ch	**ch**ur**ch**, sti**tch**	l	**l**id, need**le**, ta**ll**	th	ba**th**, **th**in
d	**d**ee**d**, mail**ed**, pu**dd**le	m	a**m**, **m**an, du**mb**	*th*	ba**the**, **th**is
		n	**n**o, sudd**en**	v	ca**v**e, val**v**e, **v**ine
f	**f**ast, **f**i**f**e, o**ff**, **ph**rase, rou**gh**	ng	thi**ng**, i**nk**	w	**w**ith, **w**olf
g	**g**a**g**, **g**et, fin**g**er	p	**p**op, ha**pp**y	y	**y**es, **y**olk, on**i**on
h	**h**at, **wh**o	r	**r**oar, **rh**yme	z	ro**s**e, si**z**e, **x**ylophone, **z**ebra
hw	**wh**ich, **wh**ere	s	mi**ss**, **s**auce, **sc**ene, **s**ee	zh	gara**g**e, plea**s**ure, vi**s**ion
j	**j**u**dg**e, **g**em	sh	di**sh**, **sh**ip, **s**ugar, ti**ss**ue		
k	**c**at, **k**i**ck**, **sch**ool				

Vowel Sounds

ă	p**a**t, l**au**gh	ŏ	h**o**rrible, p**o**t	ŭ	c**u**t, fl**oo**d, r**ou**gh, s**o**me
ā	**a**pe, **ai**d, p**ay**	ō	g**o**, r**ow**, t**oe**, th**ough**	û	c**i**rcle, f**u**r, h**ear**d, t**er**m, t**ur**n, **ur**ge, w**or**d
â	**ai**r, c**a**re, w**ea**r	ô	**a**ll, c**au**ght, f**or**, p**aw**		
ä	f**a**ther, k**o**ala, y**a**rd	oi	b**oy**, n**oi**se, **oi**l		
ĕ	p**e**t, pl**ea**sure, **a**ny	ou	c**ow**, **ou**t	yo͞o	c**u**re
ē	b**e**, b**ee**, **ea**sy, p**ia**no	o͝o	f**u**ll, b**oo**k, w**o**lf	yo͞o	ab**u**se, **u**se
ĭ	**i**f, p**i**t, b**u**sy	o͞o	b**oo**t, r**u**de, fr**ui**t, fl**ew**	ə	**a**go, sil**e**nt, penc**i**l, lem**o**n, circ**u**s
ī	r**i**de, b**y**, p**ie**, h**igh**				
î	d**ear**, d**eer**, f**ie**rce, m**ere**				

Stress Marks

Primary Stress ´: bi•ol•o•gy [bī **ŏl**´ ə jē]
Secondary Stress ˈ: bi•o•log•i•cal [bī´ ə **lŏj**´ ĭ kəl]

A

an·chor (ăng´ kər) *noun* A heavy metal object, attached to a ship, that is dropped overboard to keep the ship in place: *We dropped the **anchor** so that our sailboat wouldn't crash onto the rocky shore.*

ap·pre·ci·ate (ə prē´ shē āt´) *verb* To enjoy and understand: *Max could **appreciate** that having a dog was a big responsibility.*

a·shore (ə shôr´) *adverb* On or to the shore: *The seal came **ashore** and then went back into the water.*

B

bar·ren (băr´ ən) *adjective* Not able to produce growing plants or crops: *Because the country's land was **barren**, food had to be shipped in from other places.*

bask (băsk) *verb* To rest in a pleasant warmth: *Rochelle enjoyed the summer weather as she **basked** in the warm sun.*

buf·fet (bŭf´ ĭt) *verb* To strike against powerfully: *Luis held his kite tightly as it was **buffeted** by the strong wind.*

bur·row (bûr´ ō) *noun* A hole or tunnel small animals use as an underground nest.

bus·tling (bŭs´ lĭng) *adjective* Full of activity; busy: *The **bustling** mall was full of people shopping for holiday gifts.*

C

cease·less (sēs´ lĭs) *adjective* Continuing without end: *Kim played indoors all day because of the **ceaseless** rain.*

com·pan·ion·a·ble (kəm păn´ yən ə bəl) *adjective* Friendly: *María talked to a **companionable** girl who was sitting next to her on the train.*

cramped (krămpt) *adjective* So small as to prevent free movement: *The travelers could not stretch out their legs in the plane's **cramped** space.*

cre·vasse (krĭ văs´) *noun* A deep opening or crack: *A **crevasse** appeared in the iceberg before it broke apart.*

cus·tom (kŭs´ təm) *noun* Something that the members of a group usually do: *It is an American **custom** to eat turkey on Thanksgiving.*

burrow

Companionable

Companionable comes from the Latin word *companio*. *Com-* means "together" and *panis* means "food." Friends who share activities and sometimes eat together are companions.

crevasse

---

o͞o b**oo**t / ou **ou**t / ŭ c**u**t / û f**u**r / hw **wh**ich / th **th**in / *th* **th**is / zh vi**si**on / ə **a**go, sil**e**nt, penc**i**l, lem**o**n, circ**u**s

floe

graze

D

de·sert·ed (dĭ **zûrt´** ĕd) *adjective* Not lived in; having few or no people: *No one has lived in the **deserted** house for many years.*

dis·cour·aged (dĭ **skûr´** ĭjd) *adjective* Less hopeful or enthusiastic: *Instead of being **discouraged** by his poor grade on the test, Matt decided to study more for the next one.*

dis·mal (**dĭz´** məl) *adjective* Causing, feeling, or showing gloom or sadness: *It was a **dismal** day for Yoshiko when her best friend moved away.*

drape (drāp) *verb* To hang in loose folds: *Ellie's long skirt **draped** to the floor.*

drear·y (**drîr´** ē) *adjective* Gloomy; dismal; without cheer: *We decided not to let the **dreary** weather ruin our vacation.*

E

en·chi·la·da (ĕn´ chə **lä´** də) *noun* A tortilla that is folded around a meat filling and covered with a spicy tomato sauce: *Greg learned to make delicious chicken **enchiladas** in cooking class.*

ex·haust·ed (ĭg **zôst´** əd) *adjective* Worn out; tired: *Tina was **exhausted** after carrying the heavy boxes.*

F

fab·ric (**făb´** rĭk) *noun* Material that is produced by weaving threads, or fibers, together; cloth: *Kelly's shirt was made of a cotton **fabric**.*

floe (flō) *noun* A large, flat mass of floating ice: *The polar bear dove off the ice **floe** into the freezing water.*

for·eign·er (**fôr´** ə nər) *noun* A person from a different country or place: *Americans are **foreigners** in Europe.*

G

graze (grāz) *verb* To feed on growing plants: *The cows were **grazing** on grass near the barn.*

gru·el·ing (**groo´** ə lĭng) *adjective* Extremely tiring: *Hannah went to sleep early after running the **grueling** ten-mile race.*

H

hem (hĕm) *verb* To fold back and sew down the edge of: *I will have to **hem** my new skirt because it is too long.*

ă **r**at / ā **p**ay / â **c**are / ä **f**ather / ĕ **p**et / ē **be** / ĭ **p**it / ī **p**ie / î **f**ie**r**ce / ŏ **p**ot / ō **g**o / ô **p**aw, **fo**r / oi **oi**l / ōo **bo**ok

ho·ri·zon (hə rī´ zən) *noun*
The line along which the earth and the sky appear to meet: *Jack watched the setting sun until it disappeared below the* **horizon***.*

I

im·pass·a·ble (ĭm **păs´** ə bəl) *adjective* Impossible to travel across or through: *The mountains were* **impassable***, so we had to drive around them.*

in·stinc·tive·ly (ĭn **stĭngk´** tĭv lē) *adverb* Acting on an inner feeling that is not learned: *Most dogs* **instinctively** *try to protect their owners.*

J

jour·ney (**jûr´** nē) *noun*
Movement from one place to another; a trip: *The astronauts traveled in a spaceship during their* **journey** *to the moon.*

L

lan·guage (**lăng´** gwĭj) *noun*
Spoken or written human speech: *Jessica took a class to learn the Russian* **language***.*

launch (lônch) *verb* To send forcefully upwards like a rocket: *The swimmer pushed off the diving board before* **launching** *into the air high above the pool.*

M

mend (mĕnd) *verb* To put back into good condition; repair: *Koji couldn't wear the shirt until the rip on the sleeve was* **mended***.*

P

pass·port (**păs´** pôrt) *noun*
A government document that gives a person permission to travel in foreign countries: *Alicia needed a* **passport** *to travel to Brazil.*

pat·tern (**păt´** ərn) *noun*
An artistic design used for decoration: *The curtains have a blue striped* **pattern***.*

pelt (pĕlt) *verb* To strike or beat against again and again: *During the storm, Tomás listened to the rain* **pelting** *down on the roof.*

per·il·ous (**pĕr´** ə ləs) *adjective* Dangerous: *The icy steps were* **perilous** *to walk on.*

horizon

Language
Language comes from the Latin word *lingua*, which means "tongue."

Mend
Mend is a shortened form of the word *amend*, which means "to improve."

---

oo b**oo**t / ou **ou**t / ŭ c**u**t / û f**u**r / hw **wh**ich / th **th**in / *th* **th**is / zh vi**s**ion /
ə **a**go, sil**e**nt, penc**i**l, lem**o**n, circ**u**s

quay

skyscraper

Skyscraper

The highest sails on a ship used to be called skyscrapers. When the world's first ten-story building was built, writers called it a skyscraper, naming it after those high sails.

Strand

Strand comes from an Old English word that meant "seashore."

---

plaid (plăd) *adjective* Having a pattern formed by stripes of different widths and colors that cross each other at right angles: *Gus put on his **plaid** scarf before he went out into the cold.*

pop·u·la·tion (pŏp´ yə lā´ shən) *noun* The total number of plants, animals, or people living in a certain place: *Our class did a **population** survey to learn about the people who live in our town.*

Q

quay (kē) *noun* A dock where ships are loaded or unloaded: *The boy stood on the **quay** watching supplies being loaded onto the ships.*

R

rus·tling (rŭs´ lĭng) *noun* A soft fluttering sound: *Deb heard the **rustling** of the leaves in the wind.*

S

sal·sa (säl´ sə) *noun* A spicy sauce made of tomatoes, onions, and peppers: *We dipped our chips in the spicy **salsa**.*

seep (sēp) *verb* To pass slowly through small openings; ooze: *We stuffed a towel in the crack under the door to keep the cold air from **seeping** in.*

set·tle·ment (sĕt´l mənt) *noun* A small community in a new place: *When they reached the new land, the pioneers built a **settlement** to live in.*

sight·see·ing (sīt´ sē´ ĭng) *verb* The act of touring interesting places: *When Marc took his visitors **sightseeing** in Washington, D.C., they went to the Washington Monument.*

sky·scra·per (skī´ skrā pər) *noun* A very tall building: *The Empire State Building is one of the tallest **skyscrapers** in New York City.*

Span·ish (spăn´ ĭsh) *noun* The language of Spain, Mexico, and most of Central America and South America: *My cousin grew up in Mexico and speaks **Spanish**.*

starve (stärv) *verb* To suffer or die from lack of food: *We put seeds in the feeder so the birds wouldn't **starve** in the winter.*

strand·ed (strănd´ əd) *adjective* In a difficult or helpless position: *When our car ran out of gas, we were **stranded** on the side of the road.*

ă rat / ā pay / â care / ä father / ĕ pet / ē be / ĭ pit / ī pie / î fierce / ŏ pot /
ō go / ô paw, for / oi oil / o͝o book

sul·len·ly (**sŭl´** ən lē) *adverb*
Angrily or unhappily: *When his parents wouldn't let him have a cookie, the little boy* **sullenly** *refused to eat dinner.*

surf (sûrf) *verb* To ride on waves, often on a surfboard: *During summer vacation, Doug* **surfed** *at the beach.* —*noun* The waves of the sea as they break on a shore or reef: *Lucy swam in the* **surf**.

sur·round·ing (sə **roun´** dĭng) *adjective* On all sides of: *The* **surrounding** *trees shaded the house from the sun.*

sur·vive (sər **vīv´**) *verb* To stay alive or continue to exist: *A whale cannot* **survive** *out of water.*

swell (swĕl) *noun* A long rolling wave in open water: *The swimmer was lifted gently by the ocean* **swell**.

swoop (swōop) *verb* To move with a sudden sweeping motion: *The seagull* **swooped** *down to catch a fish.*

T

ta·co (**tä´** kō) *noun* A tortilla that is folded around a filling, such as ground meat or cheese: *We added lettuce and tomato to our* **tacos**.

ta·ma·le (tə **mä´** lē) *noun* A steamed cornhusk that is wrapped around a meat filling made with red peppers and cornmeal: *When I go to my favorite Mexican restaurant, I love to order* **tamales**.

ter·rain (tə **rān´**) *noun* Any piece of land; ground, soil, earth: *It was difficult to hike across the rocky* **terrain**.

ter·ri·to·ry (**tĕr´** ĭ tôr´ ē) *noun* An area of land; region: *Bears roam their* **territory** *in search of food.*

tor·til·la (tôr **tē´** yə) *noun* A round, flat bread made from cornmeal and water and baked on a grill: *My grandmother showed me how to make a* **tortilla**.

U

un·in·hab·i·ted (ŭn´ ĭn **hăb´** ə tĭd) *adjective* Having no people living there: *The explorer was the first person to visit the* **uninhabited** *island.*

V

vend·or (**vĕn´** dər) *noun* A person who sells something: *In Chicago, Carl bought a hot dog from a street* **vendor**.

surf

Terrain
Terrain comes from the Latin word *terra*, which means "earth." Other words that come from *terra* are *territory*, *terrace*, and *terrier*.

vendor

ōō b**oo**t / ou **ou**t / ŭ c**u**t / û f**u**r / hw **wh**ich / th **th**in / *th* **th**is / zh vi**s**ion /
ə **a**go, sil**e**nt, penc**i**l, lem**o**n, circ**u**s

419

venture

ven·ture (**vĕn´** chər) *verb* To do something in spite of risk: *We decided to **venture** out to the edge of the cliff.*

W

wan·der (**wŏn´** dər) *verb* To move from place to place without a special purpose or goal: *People in shopping malls often **wander** from store to store.*

wea·ry (**wîr´** ē) *adjective* Needing rest; tired: *After climbing the mountain, the **weary** hikers took a nap.*

ă rat / ā pay / â care / ä father / ĕ pet / ē be / ĭ pit / ī pie / î fierce / ŏ pot / ō go / ô paw, for / oi oil / ŏŏ book

Acknowledgments

Pronunciation key and definitions © 1998 by Houghton Mifflin Company. Adapted and reprinted by permission from The American Heritage Children's Dictionary.

Main Literature Selections

Across the Wide Dark Sea: The Mayflower Journey, by Jean Van Leeuwen, illustrated by Thomas B. Allen. Text copyright © 1995 by Jean Van Leeuwen. Illustrations copyright © 1995 by Thomas B. Allen. Reprinted by permission of Dial Books for Young Readers, a division of Penguin Books Inc.

Alejandro's Gift, by Richard E. Albert, illustrated by Sylvia Long. Text copyright © 1994 by Richard E. Albert. Illustrations copyright © 1994 by Sylvia Long. Reprinted by permission of the publisher, Chronicle Books LLC, San Francisco. Visit http://www.chroniclebooks.com.

"Helen Keller" from *Sisters in Strength,* by Yona Zeldis McDonough, illustrated by Malcah Zeldis. Text copyright © 2000 by Yona Zeldis McDonough. Reprinted by permission of Henry Holt and Company, LLC.

The Island-Below-the-Star, written and illustrated by James Rumford. Copyright © 1998 by James Rumford. Reprinted by permission of Houghton Mifflin Company. All rights reserved.

Nights of the Pufflings, by Bruce McMillan. Copyright © 1995 by Bruce McMillan. Reprinted by permission of Houghton Mifflin Company. All rights reserved.

Pepita Talks Twice/Pepita habla dos veces, by Ofelia Dumas Lachtman. Copyright © 1995 by Ofelia Dumas Lachtman. Reprinted with permission from the publisher Arte Publico Press/University of Houston.

Poppa's New Pants, by Angela Shelf Medearis, illustrated by John Ward. Text copyright © 1995 by Angela Shelf Medearis. Illustrations copyright © 1995 by John Ward. Reprinted by permission of Holiday House, Inc.

Selection from *Prairie School,* by Avi. Text copyright © 2001 by Avi. Reprinted by permission of HarperCollins Publishers.

Selection from *Ramona Quimby, Age 8,* by Beverly Cleary, illustrated by Alan Tiegreen. Copyright © 1981 by Beverly Cleary. Reprinted by permission of HarperCollins Publishers.

Seal Surfer, by Michael Foreman. Copyright © 1996 by Michael Foreman. Reprinted by permission of Harcourt Inc.

Trapped by the Ice!: Shackleton's Amazing Antarctic Adventure, by Michael McCurdy. Copyright © 1997 by Michael McCurdy. Reprinted by arrangement with Walker & Co.

Two Days in May, by Harriet Peck Taylor, pictures by Leyla Torres. Text copyright © 1999 by Harriet Peck Taylor. Illustrations copyright © 1999 by Leyla Torres. Reprinted by permission of Farrar, Straus and Giroux, LLC.

"A Wild Ride," by Thomas Fleming, from the March 2002 issue of *Boy's Life* magazine. Text copyright © 2002 by Thomas Fleming. Cover copyright © 2002 by the Boy Scouts of America. Reprinted by permission of the author and Boy's Life, published by the Boy Scouts of America.

Yunmi and Halmoni's Trip, by Sook Nyul Choi, illustrated by Karen Dugan. Text copyright © 1997 by Sook Nyul Choi. Illustrations copyright © 1997 by Karen Dugan. Reprinted by permission of Houghton Mifflin Company. All rights reserved.

Focus Selections

Cinderella, by Charles Perrault, retold by Amy Ehrlich. Text copyright © 1985 by Amy E. Ehrlich. Published by arrangement with Dial Books for Young Readers, a member of Penguin Putnam Inc.

Selection from *Yeh-Shen: A Cinderella Story from China,* retold by Ai-Ling Louie, illustrated by Ed Young. Text copyright © 1982 by Ai-Ling Louie. Illustrations copyright © 1982 by Ed Young. Reprinted by permission of Philomel Books, a division of Penguin Young Readers Group, a member of Penguin Group (USA) Inc. Electronic rights granted by the author for the text and by McIntosh and Otis, Inc. for the illustrations. All rights reserved.

of Random House, Inc. and the author.
"Young Voyagers: A Pilgrim Childhood."
Grateful acknowledgment is given to the
Plimoth Plantation for the printed resource
materials that were provided for informational
purposes.

Additional Acknowledgments
Special thanks to the following teachers whose
students' compositions appear as Student Writing
Models: Cindy Cheatwood, Florida; Diana Davis,
North Carolina; Kathy Driscoll, Massachusetts;
Linda Evers, Florida; Heidi Harrison, Michigan;
Eileen Hoffman, Massachusetts; Bonnie Lewison,
Florida; Kanetha McCord, Michigan.

Credits

Photography
1 (t) © Royalty-Free/Corbis. (m) V.C.L./Taxi/
Getty Images. (b) © JIStock/Masterfile. **3** ©
Royalty-Free/Corbis. **4** (l) Corbis/Bettmann.
(m) Jeff Arnold/Bill Melendez Productions. (r)
AP/New York Times Pictures. **6** V.C.L./Taxi/
Getty Images. **9** © JIStock/Masterfile. **10–11**
©Michio Hoshino/Minden Pictures. **11** (m) ©
Royalty-Free/Corbis. **12–14** Courtesy of
Bruce McMillan. **16–17** (bkgd) ©Hubert
Stadler/CORBIS. **17** (t) ©Sigurgeir Jonasson.
(b) ©James P. Rowan. **18** (tc) Benner McGee,
©1995 Bruce McMillan. **18-19** (bkgd) ©
Catherine Karow/ Corbis. **19–33** ©Bruce
McMillan. **35** (br) Arthur C. Smith III/Grant
Heilman. **36–9** (all) ©Arthur Morris/BIRDS
AS ART. **40** ©Kit Kittle/CORBIS. **41** ©Clem
Haagner; Gallo Images/CORBIS. **42** ©Lynda
Richardson/ CORBIS. **43** (t) ©James L. Amos/
CORBIS. **44** (starfish) © PhotoDisc/Getty
Images. (c) ©Rick Rusing/Stone/Getty Images.
(bl) ©Roger Tidman/CORBIS. **44–5** ©Bill
Ross/CORBIS. **45** (cl) ©Art Wolfe. (br) ©Phil
Schermeister/CORBIS. **46** ©Ron Sutherland.
46-47 (bkgd) © Doug Wilson/Corbis. **65** (br)
A.K.G., Berlin/SuperStock. **66–9** (all)
©Norbert Wu. **70** (banner) W. Cody/
CORBIS. (bl) ©Erwin and Peggy Bauer. **70–1**
©Daniel J. Cox/Natural Exposures.
71 (inset) ©Daniel J. Cox/Natural Exposures.
72-73 (bkgd) © Bohemian Nomad
Picturemakers/Corbis. **93** (bl) John Crispin/

Mercury Pictures. (tr) Eric Bakke/Mercury
Pictures. **100-11** (bkgd) © Joseph Van Os/The
Image Bank/Getty Images. **100** (b) © Royalty-
Free/Corbis. **114–16** (border) Corbis Images/
Picturequest. **115** (bkgd) Larry Ulrich/DRK
Photo, (tl) Francois Gohier/Photo Researchers,
Inc., (bl) Craig Lorenz/Photo Researchers, Inc.
116 (t) Stephen Krasemann/Photo Researchers,
Inc., (b) Rod Planck. **122**Corbis/Bettmann.
123 Corbis/Bettmann. **124** Corbis/Bettmann.
125 (t) Corbis/Bettmann. (b) Underwood &
Underwood/CORBIS. **126** (tr) AP/Wide
World Photos. (bl) Corbis/Bettmann. **127**
Zaharias Collection, Special Collections/Mary
& John Gray Library/Lamar University,
Beaumont, Texas. **128** Jeff Arnold/Bill
Meléndez Productions. **129** Photofest. **130** ©
PhotoDisc/Getty Images. **131** Photofest. **132**
Photofest. **133** Everett Collection. **134**
Underwood & Underwood/CORBIS. **135**
Security Pacific Collection/Los Angeles Public
Library. **136** CORBIS. **137** Museum of
Flight/CORBIS. **138** The Lilly Library,
Indiana University, Bloomington. **139** USPS.
140 Corbis/Bettmann. **141** AP/New York
Times Pictures. **142** Corbis/Bettmann. **143**
AP/New York Times Pictures. **144** AP Wide
World Photos. **145** (t) Corbis/Bettmann. (b)
AP/Wide World Photos. **146** (l) AFP/Corbis.
(cl) Flip Schulke/CORBIS. (cr) NASA/
CORBIS. (r) Corbis/Bettmann. **148-49** (bkgd)
© Kelly Harriger/CORBIS. **149** (m) V.C.L./
Taxi/Getty Images. **150–51** Courtesy of Sook
Nyul Choi. **152** (t) Courtesy of Manhattanville
College, (b) Courtesy of Sook Nyul Choi. **154**
(bl) Courtesy of the Pilgrim Society, Plymouth,
Massachusetts. **155** (t) Photo by Bert Lane/
Plimoth Plantation. (b) Courtesy of the Pilgrim
Society, Plymouth, Massachusetts. **156** (tl)
Photo by David Gavril from Growing Ideas
published by Richard C. Owens Publishers,
Inc., Katonah, NY 10536. (tr) Courtesy,
Thomas B. Allen. **156-57** (bkgd) Kaz Mori/
The Image Bank/Getty Images. **179** (br)
SuperStock. **182** (tl) Photo by Ted
Curtain/Plimoth Plantation. (b) Photo by Ted
Avery/Plimoth Plantation. **183** (t) ©Dorothy
Littell Greco/Stock Boston. (c) (b) ©Russ
Kendall. **186** (b) ©Wolfgang Kaehler/

CORBIS. **187** (tl) (br) ©Kevin R. Morris/ CORBIS. **188** (t) Jesse Nemerofsky/Mercury Pictures (b)Courtesy, Karen Dugan. **188-89** (bkgd) Bob Thomas/Stone/Getty Images. **210** Geese in Flight, Leila T. Bauman, Gift of Edgar William and Bernice Chrystler Garbisch, ©2000 Board of Trustees, National Gallery of Art, Washington. **211** Giraudon/Art Resource, New York. **212** Erich Lessing/Art Resource, New York. **213** (t) Scala/Art Resource, New York. (b) Art Resource, New York. **214** (banner) © G. Ryan & S. Beyer/Stone/Getty Images. (tr) Scott Polar Research Institute, Cambridge, England. **215** ©Galen Rowell/ Mountain Light. **216** Courtesy, Michael McCurdy. **216-17** (bkgd) ©Shanker/Stock Image/Panoramic Images. **246** (bl) © PhotoDisc/Getty Images **247** (bl) SuperStock. **248** (tr) Scott Polar Research Institute, Cambridge, England. (b) ©Royal Geographical Society, London. **249** Scott Polar Research Institute, Cambridge, England. **250** (tl) ©Royal Geographical Society, London. (cl) ©Royal Geographical Society, London. **250-1** (b) ©Royal Geographical Society, London. (t) Scott Polar Research Institute, Cambridge, England. **251** (c) ©Royal Geographical Society, London. **252-3** (bkgd) Digital Vision/Getty Images. **252** (b) V.C.L./ Taxi/Getty Images. **262** Culver Pictures. **263** (mr) Culver Pictures. **264** (tr) Time Life Pictures/Getty Images. **296-7** (bkgd) © Zigy Kaluzny/Stone/Getty Images. **297** (m) © JIStock/Masterfile. **298** Courtesy of Ofelia Dumas Lachtman. **302** (b) Power Photos. **303** (cl) ©Eric and David Hosking/ CORBIS. (bl) Corbis Royalty Free. (br) © PhotoDisc/Getty Images **304** (tl) Michael Justice/Mercury Pictures. (tr) Courtesy, Mike Reed. **304-5** (bkgd) © Barry Winiker/Index Stock Imagery/ PictureQuest. **342** (t) Andrew Yates/Mercury Pictures. (b) ©Tom Sciacca. **342-3** (bkgd) © M. Angelo/Corbis. **370** (t) Alan McEwen, 1999. (b) M. W. Thomas. **370-1** (bkgd) Stephen Simpson/Taxi/Getty Images. **400-1** (bkgd) © Zigy Kaluzny/Stone/Getty Images. **400** (b) © JIStock/Masterfile. **402–404** Courtesy of the American Foundation for the

Blind, Helen Keller Archives. **405** (ml) Courtesy of Perkins School for the Blind, (mr) Hulton–Deutsch Collection/Corbis. **415** (t) ©Kevin Schafer/CORBIS. (b) ©Lowell Georgia/CORBIS. **416** (t) ©Dan Guravich/ CORBIS. (b) ©Darrell Gulin/CORBIS. **417** ©Gary Braasch/CORBIS. **418** (t) ©Judy Griesedieck/CORBIS. (b) ©Kit Kittle/ CORBIS. **419** (t) ©Tony Arruza/CORBIS. (b) ©Catherine Karnow/CORBIS. **420** ©Kevin R. Morris/ CORBIS.

Assignment Photography

34 (bl), **35** (ml), **64** (bl), **65** (ml), **95** (ml), **178** (b), **179** (ml), **209** (ml, mr), **247** (mr), **333** (tr), **368** (ml, mr), **394** (bl) Jack Holtel. **119, 267, 413** © HMCo./Michael Indresano Photography **303** (tr) Tony Scarpetta. **303** (tl) Banta Digital Group. **340-1, 368-9, 397-9** Joel Benjamin.

Illustration

93 Dick Cole. **96–99** Normand Cousineau. **120-21** Sandra Spiegel. **150** (Colorized photo) Walter Stuart. **151** (b) Joe LeMonnier, (Colorized photo) Walter Stuart. **152** (Colorized photo) Walter Stuart. **180-81, 182-3** (bkgd) Luigi Galante. **264** (border) Frank Riccio. **268-69** Robert Sauber. **298–301** Viviana Garofoli. **305** (i) Alex Pardo DeLange. **306-31** Mike Reed. **334-5** Karen Blessen. **371** (i), **372-93** Alan Tiegreen. **407–410** Stacey Schuett.